YVE BLAKE is a composer, lyricist, playwright and screenwriter born on the lands of the Eora Nation (Sydney, Australia). She is best known for writing the book, music and lyrics for the smash-hit musical *FANGIRLS*. In 2019, *FANGIRLS* premiered at Queensland Theatre and Belvoir to multiple five-star reviews and sell-out crowds, and in 2021 it returned by popular demand for an Australian tour. *FANGIRLS* was awarded the 2019 Sydney Theatre Award for Best Mainstage Musical, the Matilda Award for Best Musical or Cabaret, and received the 2020 AWGIE award for Music Theatre. Previously, Yve has had her work developed and presented at Soho Theatre, Southbank Centre, Old Vic New Voices, the National Theatre Studio, The Barbican, Griffin Theatre Company and the Brisbane Powerhouse. She was the inaugural recipient of the atyp Rebel Wilson Theatre-Maker Scholarship, is an alumni of the Royal Court Writers' Programme, and has also been a visiting artist at Princeton University. In 2019, Yve took the stage in front of five and a half thousand people as a speaker at TEDxSydney. Her talk 'For the love of *Fangirls*' has since been promoted to an official TED talk on TED.com, where it has received more than a million views. Currently, Yve is developing several other new works for stage, film, TV and podcast audio.

From left: Chika Ikogwe, Sharon Millerchip, Yve Blake, James Majoos, Ayesha Madon and Kimberley Hodgson in the QT / Brisbane Festival / Belvoir 2019 co-production. (Photo: Brett Boardman)

FANGIRLS

YVE BLAKE

CURRENCY PRESS
The performing arts publisher

CURRENCY PLAYS

First published in 2021
by Currency Press Pty Ltd,
Gadigal Land, Suite 310, 46-56 Kippax Street, Surry Hills NSW 2010
enquiries@currency.com.au
www.currency.com.au

Reprinted 2021, 2023, 2024

Typeset by Dean Nottle for Currency Press.
Printed by CanPrint Communications, Canberra, ACT.
Cover image by Alphabet Studio.
Cover design by Emma Vine for Currency Press.
Cover shows Yve Blake.
Currency Press acknowledges the Traditional Owners of the Country on which we live and work. We pay our respects to all Aboriginal and Torres Strait Islander Elders, past and present.

A catalogue record for this book is available from the National Library of Australia

Contents

FANGIRLS was developed and produced across Australia on the lands of the Gadigal, Wangal and Bidjigal people of the Eora Nation, the Wurundjeri and Boon Wurrung peoples, the Kaurna people, the Wonnarua people, and the Jagera and Turrbal people. We, the creators, acknowledge each of these as the Traditional Custodians of the lands on which we were privileged to craft this work. We pay our deepest respects to their Elders past and present, as well as to all First Nations peoples across Australia. Sovereignty was never ceded. These lands always were, and always will be, Aboriginal lands.

Enough warmth, witty lines and catchy tunes to win its own fangirls

Comedy often succeeds where tragedy fails. *FANGIRLS* is not the first drama to explore our fascination with the wild, uncontrollable power of young female passion and girls' infatuation with their boy-loves. Yet its catchy tunes, witty dialogue, and hilarious, occasionally absurdist, comic scenes set it apart.

Over 2,500 years ago, Euripides' play *The Bacchae* featured a chorus of *maenads*, followers of Dionysus and the world's first fangirls, who ecstatically tore cattle apart with their bare hands. Any unfortunate male who crossed their path was similarly rendered limb from limb. Fear of uninhibited female obsession runs deep.

Stephen King's *Misery*, starring the psychotic uber-fan Annie Wilkes (Kathy Bates), struck a chord in our collective psyche. The delusional female fan has long been a character to be feared and shunned. At best a figure of derision, at worst a figure in need of strong medical and psychiatric intervention.

It is against this background that *FANGIRLS* seems so refreshing. This musical doesn't stigmatise the world of the fangirl and her pop-star fixations, it revels in it. It emerges from a genuine desire to understand and celebrate its subject. Driven by such compassion, the laughs—and there are many—are never cheap.

The musical teaches us that the boundless creativity of young girls needs to run free, not be stifled by convention or ideas of proper behaviour. Armed with unbreakable determination and a few instructional YouTube clips these girls can achieve anything. The bouncy, upbeat music and dynamic video-walls that dominate the stage capture well the frenzied energy unleashed by the fangirl. Whatever it is, idol worship is not idle worship.

The story and music were written by the abundantly talented Yve Blake who plays the lead role of young 14-year-old Edna [in the first production]. The plot of the musical concerns Edna and her fixation on Harry (AYDAN), the lead singer of the world's biggest boy band True

Connection. With smouldering eyes and perfect hair, Harry's effect on his teenage fanbase is visceral.

In an early musical number, Harry's fans writhe around in half-agony, half-ecstasy clutching their pillowcases as they remember the first time that they witnessed him take the stage. As a former star of the hit talent show 'The Voice', Aydan is perfectly suited to the role.

Edna's devotion to Harry and her unshakeable conviction that only she truly understands him is a source of tension between Edna, her school friends and her mother (Sharon Millerchip). Edna escapes from her increasingly fraught home life through the internet and the chatrooms full of True Connection fans.

Together with her online BFF Saltypringl, brilliantly played by James Majoos, Edna writes fan fiction in which she and Saltypringl imagine scenarios where they each team up with Harry to fight against their common enemies. The opponents become increasingly outrageous, but the trajectory of the stories remains the same. With the opposition out of the way, Edna and Saltypringl can each enjoy time alone with Harry as they giddily tousle those begging-to-be-played-with locks. Gradually the line between fiction and reality becomes blurred with literally riotous results.

In the hands of another dramatist, Edna could be a figure to be pitied. In *FANGIRLS*, you constantly cheer her on, no matter how ridiculous her plans. Her friends may treat her badly, but you forgive them as well. They possess such vitality and spunk that most crimes can be forgiven.

Edna's frenemy Jules (Chika Ikogwe) is so fabulous in her narcissism that you forget all of the terrible things she says and does. In all her naked unrestrained power she is a joy to behold.

This musical neatly exposes the gender double standard that lies at the heart of our treatment of fangirls. We mock them for their exuberance, but if a boy showed similar passion for a footballer or cricketer, we wouldn't hesitate to applaud such devotion.

It equally reveals the cynicism of the commercial music industry that seeks to atomise its fanbase. The songs of boy bands claim to be speaking to you alone. Anyone else who thinks otherwise is delusional. It is an irresponsible strategy that promotes intense rivalries, online trolling, and fights between fans. Boy bands cause division as much as they unite.

The scenes of teenage life are painfully well observed and many parents will wince in recognition of how Edna speaks to her mother. Yet it is the warmth of the drama that shines through. This musical is a celebration of love in all its forms. It is a reminder that it is love that makes us better people, repairs shattered friendships, and teaches us to appreciate life. It is love, not some pop star—no matter how perfect the hair—that makes us whole.

Alastair Blanshard

This article first appeared in *The Conversation* in September 2019 as a review to the Queensland Theatre / Brisbane Festival / Belvoir co-production. Alastair Blanshard is the Paul Eliadis Chair of Classics and Ancient History at the University of Queensland.

From left: Kimberley Hodgson, Yve Blake, James Majoos, Ayesha Madon (back to camera), Chika Ikogwe and AYDAN (on screen) in the QT / Brisbane Festival / Belvoir 2019 co-production. (Photo: Brett Boardman)

DIRECTOR'S NOTE

FANGIRLS is a celebration of young women, their passion and their power. It has a narrative that we are not often told, that if they put their mind to it, teenage girls can achieve anything.

If watching 16-year-old Greta Thunberg address the UN the week we started rehearsals for the premiere season was anything to go by, the world needed to brace itself, because the myths teenage girls have been sold for so long—that they're 'weak' and 'hysterical', that their love and passion is 'crazy'—were being dismantled rapidly. With *FANGIRLS*, Yve Blake is contributing to that disruption whilst simultaneously injecting joy and understanding and love into the world by the bucketload.

A brilliant team over many years helped Yve create *FANGIRLS*, it was developed over five years in total, the core team being Yve with Jonathan Ware as dramaturg, David Muratore as music producer/ sound designer and the glorious Alice Chance as the vocal arranger and music director. Watching these four very talented artists work was such a pleasure, their dedication, drive and belief in each other and themselves was incredibly inspiring.

I joined the team around two years before we began rehearsals and assembled another creative team around that core—David Fleischer, Justin Harrison, Leonard Mickelo, Emma Valente and Michael Waters. Their generosity and sheer brilliance allowed the show to sparkle in the way it deserved to. Then came our cast. They impressed us at every turn—the boundless energy and precision, creative contribution and pure talent was the greatest pleasure to work with. It has been the only production I've worked on to date that gave me more energy than I gave it. We recently had a development in preparation for our return 2021 season and new cast members have joined. They are as talented, joyous and energetic as the last. I'm constantly impressed by the emerging talent in our industry, especially when working on *FANGIRLS*.

It's important I acknowledge some more people (the team is huge!). This production wouldn't have happened without our original stage management team of Bella Kurdijk and Katie Moore. Huge thanks also to our associate director Carissa Licciardello, Louise Gough for additional dramaturgy and our voice and dialect coach Amy Hume. The production and technical team on this show went above and beyond—Gareth/Chris, Dan/Toni and their teams and of course the staff at Belvoir, Queensland Theatre and ATYP. They all deserve their own celebratory concert medleys!

I'm so pleased *FANGIRLS* has been gifted another life in 2021. The positivity and love that pours from this production is the perfect antidote to what has been and continues to be such a difficult time worldwide and I seriously can't wait to see school productions of this wonderful beast. It is a gift to any who are lucky enough to experience it, whether it's through watching, reading, listening or working on it—*FANGIRLS*, like Harry's hair, gives life.

Paige Rattray
Director

ACKNOWLEDGEMENTS

Thank you to Rebel Wilson, ATYP, Global Creatures, The Barbican Open Lab, Women of the World Festival, Adelaide Cabaret Festival, Belvoir, Queensland Theatre, and Brisbane Festival for giving me the resources to develop this show.

Thank you to Ella Camille, Dominica Nichols, Kelly Jonske and Lizzie Curran for the research assistance. To Amy Maiden, who fought hard for this show before anyone cared about it. To Jenni Medway, Jane FitzGerald and Louise Gough for your dramaturgical input and meaningful encouragement. Thank you to every SINGLE performer who generously helped to develop this work, you all deserve a shout out: Adam Sollis, Alex Watson, Angus Wilkinson, Aydan Califiore, Ayesha Madon, Bardiya McKinnon, Baylie Carson, Brooke McElligot, Callan Purcell, Carly Mercedes Dyer, Chika Ikogwe, Claudia Pereira, Contessa Treffone, Daniel Gabriel, Daniel Hamilton, Ella Moeck, Elysia Hall, Emilia Higgs, Emma Jackson, Emma O'Sullivan, Grace Royle, Hannah Barlow, Hannah Coombes, Hilary Cole, James Majoos, Janet Anderson, Jaqui McLaren, Jessica King, Jessica Vickers, Jim Fishwick, Joshua McElroy, Josie Gibson, Jules Orcullo, Julia Rorke, Kate Allt, Kate Cheel, Kimberley Hodgson, Kirsty Marillier, Laura Kaye Thomson, Liz Buchanan, Lucy Coleman, Lucy Green, Marney McQueen, Melissa Russo, Mychelle Scott, Nancy Dennis, Paige McKay, Rachel Burke, Sam Clark, Sanne Baltus, Sharon Millerchip, Simon Croker, Sofia Barclay, Stef Johnston, Stephanie Zuzolo, Taylor Anthony, and Tom Anson Mesker, I AM INDEBTED TO YOU!

Thank you to my team, Claire Nightingale, Avi Lipski, Marilen Tabacco, Clare Mirabello and the unstoppable Michael Lynch. To Tim Minchin, Adam Lenson, Jules Patey, Phil Jameson, Ali McGregor, Alex Groves, Scott Quinn, Thomas Wilson-White, Georgia Symons, Clotilde De Verteuil and Lachlan Philpott—you all know what you did. To the original cast and creative team, for making this show more extra than I could have ever dreamed. To Paige Rattray, for being my dream director and fierce protector. You are an actual genius.

And most of all, thank you Johnny, Dave and Alice. We've grown up together making this. You began as my collaborators and you became my muses. Thank you for this adventure.

P.S. Mum, Dad, Furby and Caroline: This is dedicated to you.

Yve Blake

A note from the author

Since this text was first published, I decided to edit two lines in this show, and mates—I want to be up front about it! On pages 25 and 83, the character of Jules used to make some intentionally toxic comments about fatness. When I first wrote these lines, it was 2016, and I was hoping to make a point about all the ways that the world brainwashes young people into fearing that they're not enough, but with time, I felt that the comments were instead just reinforcing some ideas I don't agree with. All bodies rule!

Yve Blake, 2024

FANGIRLS was first produced by Belvoir and Queensland Theatre in association with Brisbane Festival and Australian Theatre for Young People, on 12 September 2019, at the Bille Brown Theatre, Queensland Theatre, with the following cast:

EDNA	Yve Blake
HARRY	AYDAN
BRIANNA	Kimberley Hodgson
JULES	Chika Ikogwe
SALTYPRINGL	James Majoos
CAROLINE	Sharon Millerchip
LILY	Ayesha Madon
SWING PERFORMER	Melissa Russo

Book, Music and Lyrics, Yve Blake
Director, Paige Rattray
Vocal Arranger / Music Director, Alice Chance
Music Producer / Sound Designer, David Muratore
Dramaturg, Jonathan Ware
Set, Video Content and Costume Designer, David Fleischer
Lighting Designer, Emma Valente
Associate Lighting Designer, Ben Hughes
Video Content Design and Production, Justin Harrison
Choreographer, Leonard Mickelo
Sound Designer, Michael Waters
Associate Director, Carissa Licciardello
Stage Manager, Isabella Kerdijk
Assistant Stage Manager, Katie Moore
Voice / Dialect Coach, Amy Hume

CHARACTERS

EDNA, 14. A misfit. Lovably awkward. Fiercely intelligent. Wild imagination. Lives in a tiny flat with her single mum. Hates superficiality. Loves Harry.

JULES, 14, but thinks she's 21. Obsessed with boys. Wants to always be in control. Secretly terrified of being abandoned.

BRIANNA, 14. She'll snort-laugh at your jokes even when they're not funny. Uncomfortable in her body. Hates conflict.

CAROLINE, Edna's mum. Works night shifts as a nurse to make ends meet. Tired. Loves Edna more than anything. Thinks True Connection (Harry's band) is problematic.

HARRY, 18. He's the clear favourite in the world's biggest boy band; True Connection. British Midlands accent. Breathtakingly gorgeous. Hair that 'gives you life'.

THE FANS

These characters might all live in different cities / have different accents.

LILY, 13. Radiates sweetness until she's angry, then she might actually kill you. Can riff like Mariah Carey.

ASH, A kid. Comically earnest. For her, loving Harry actually hurts.

DOM, teens. Horny for Harry. A bit goth.

GRETA, teens. An enthusiastic dork. Spectacularly uncoordinated.

SALTYPRINGL, A queer fanboy (or nonbinary kid) who is friends with Edna through the internet (and who lives in a different country from Edna). The internet is the only place where Salty can be him/themself, and being in the fandom gets Salty through life. Ultimately, Salty just wants to make the world a better place.

OTHER CHARACTERS

ROSA, CAM, TAL, NAZ, fans who live in the same city as Edna

RIWA, a fan in Tasmania

YAEL, GEORGIA, two fans who are hyper and naughty

COP 1, experienced cop

COP 2, rookie cop

VIDEO CHARACTERS

In the original production, the following characters appeared in videos that were projected on enormous LED screens that formed the show's set. In other productions, they could also appear live:

VIDEO FAN CHORUS

NEWSREADERS

HARRY'S MUM

RADIO BRO

SUE CRELLEN

MEMBERS OF THE BAND TRUE CONNECTION

REES, the bad boy

ZAK, the buff one

LEO, the sensitive one

MYLES, the prankster

CAST

The original production was performed by a cast of seven, with roles distributed as follows:

EDNA / TRUE CONNECTION MEMBER

HARRY

JULES / GRETA / CAM / COP 1 / TRUE CONNECTION MEMBER

BRIANNA / DOM / COP 2 / TRUE CONNECTION MEMBER

CAROLINE / ASH / TAL / TRUE CONNECTION MEMBER

SALTY / ROSA / YAEL

LILY / RIWA / GEORGIA / NAZ

The company was expanded to a cast of nine for the 2021 tour.

NOTES FOR READERS

/ indicates a cue to overlap the next line

[ ] indicates either a stage direction or an idea or place that can be localised per venue

dialogue in **bold** indicates lyrics / sung text.

From left: Kimberley Hodgson, James Majoos and Sharon Millerchip in the QT / Brisbane Festival / Belvoir 2019 co-production. (Photo: Brett Boardman)

ACT ONE

SCENE 1—A DARK ALLEYWAY—NIGHT

The sound of police sirens fills the space. Two COPS *run on with flashlights.*

COP 1: You sure he went this way?

COP 2: It looked like him.

COP 1: [*into his chest radio, annoyed*] Alley is clear. He's not here.

RADIO: [*voice-over*] Any sign of the girl?

COP 1: [*into his chest radio*] Nowhere. They're probably on the road by now.

RADIO: [*voice-over*] I'll get the choppers on it.

COP 1: [*to* COP 2] C'mon, newbie.

COP 1 *exits.* COP 2 *begins to follow, but then she sees it: a big bin.*

Alone now, she kicks it. She lifts the lid when …

EDNA *pops out of it. She pounces on* COP 2 *and clamps a hand over her screaming mouth. They struggle.* COP 2 *manages to throw* EDNA *to the ground.*

But then, HARRY *appears, holding a knife. He grabs* COP 2 *and stabs her repeatedly. She crumples.* HARRY *lifts her limp body over his shoulder.*

HARRY: Bin!

EDNA *holds the bin steady while* HARRY *folds* COP 2*'s body into it. Sirens sound.*

Run.

Hand in hand, they run. Strings swell up.

Instantly they appear elsewhere. Safe now. As they sing to each other, they dance a duet. This is the most intense young love you've ever seen. It's hot.

SONG: 'LET THEM'

VERSE 1

EDNA: **I was. Waiting. For my life to begin**
Homesick. For a place. I had never been

In just one look, I realised.
I found that place, was in your eyes
And now I'll never feel alone again

VERSE 2

HARRY: **Fake smiles. Tight chest. Trapped in his own skin**
EDNA: **You were just like me**
HARRY: **Dreamt of. Running. From everything that was 'him'**
EDNA: **I had to set you free**
HARRY: **In just one look, could not deny**
EDNA: **Without me you've only**
Been half alive
HARRY: **Without you, I've only**
Been half alive
HARRY & EDNA: **Now I'll never feel alone again**

PRE-CHORUS

Let them all say we're wrong
Let's leave them in our dust
'Cause now the only real thing …

They giggle.

An epic CHOIR *joins them.*

CHORUS 1

EDNA: **Is us**
Just us
Just us
Uu-u-u-us
Uu-u-u-us
Just uuuuuu—

HARRY: **Is uuuuus**
Just us

Starts riffing impressively.

Baby, you know it's just u-u-u-us
You set me fre-e-e-ee
And I will never let you go, no-o-o-o
Just uuuuuu—

Right as they're about to kiss:

SCENE 2—EDNA'S BEDROOM

CAROLINE: [*calling from offstage*] EDNAAA?

The music cuts. EDNA *and* HARRY *look at each other, horrified.*

Edna's mum, CAROLINE, *calls through her bedroom door.*

Edna? Dinner's in five—

EDNA: I'M BUSY, MUM!

Snap: we are in Edna's bedroom. EDNA *is at her laptop, a pop song blaring out of her headphones.* CAROLINE *bursts in.*

CAROLINE: What are you looking at?

EDNA: Homework! Mum! CAN YOU KNOCK?!

CAROLINE: Well. Come get some dinner.

EDNA: I will later, Mum, I'm just REALLY busy.

EDNA *puts her headphones on.*

CAROLINE: Ed— [*Lifting a headphone*] C'mon, I wanna hear about your day before I leave for work.

EDNA: MUM! I have homework! Do you want me to lose my scholarship?! OH MY GOD?!

EDNA*'s headphones blare. She ignores* CAROLINE.

CAROLINE: Ed? … Okay. See you in the morning.

CAROLINE *goes. Behind her back,* EDNA *pulls a frustrated face at her mum. She refocuses on her laptop and begins to type feverishly.*

A deep bass sound rumbles. The sound of whispering teenage girls spins around us, and rises into the sound of a church organ.

SCENE 3—NOBODY

A choir of girls sings angelically. LILY *appears tightly lit. She looks about eleven.*

SONG: 'NOBODY'

INTRO

LILY: **I was ten when it happened**
Never been the same
Now I know why they call it a crush

[*100 mph*] 'Cause your insides feel smushed like a building fell on you or like your lower intestines are being pulled out like they're tooth floss, and your belly button is a tooth floss box and it hurts and it's like seriously can you just stop it though-a!

[*At anyone who laughed*] … It's not funny!

The CHOIR *flourishes.*

But it's a warm and fuzzy pain ohhh

For each solo, a new FAN *is tightly lit.*

VERSE 1

ASH: **I couldn't eat**
GRETA: **I couldn't stop eating**
LILY: **I couldn't sleep**
SALTY: **I just couldn't even**
GRETA: **You give me hand sweat**
DOM: **You're a kick to the head**
LILY: **Your smile gives me life**
SALTY: **Your hair kills me dead**
ASH: **Your face strobes in my mind**
You're every second thought, I can't get you out
LILY: **When I'm home alone I talk to you**
DOM: **I'm caught like a fish**
GRETA: **You're like a hook through my mouth!**

CHORUS 1

ASH: **You make me feel different**
LILY: **You make me feel real**
DOM: **This love has changed me**
SALTY: **You make me feel ALL THE FEELS**
EDNA: **Because in your eyes I'm someone**
I wanna beeeeeee

[*Whispered*] Harry!

As they sing this line, the FANS *all reveal merch covered in Harry's face.*

ALL: **HA-A-ARRY**
EDNA: **Nobody loves you like m—**

ALL: **MEEEEEEEEEEEEEEE**

Percussion kicks in. The FANS *interrupt each other, bursting with feels.*

VERSE 2

SALTY: **Two years ago,**
History turned a new page, when
On a British talent show, a nervous boy
Walked onstage and—
ASH: **He's fifteen**
He's from Cheshire
LILY: **That's his mum's cardigan!**
DOM: **He hates mayonnaise!**
GRETA: **ME TOO!**
SALTY: **But, we didn't know that then.**
LILY: **When suddenly the**
Searing screams
Stopped

The FANS *are frozen in wonder. We hear the sound of a beating heart. They sing angelically:*

CHORUS 2

DOM: **He opened his mouth**
DOM & LILY: **And opened our eyes**
SALTY & ASH: **A voice so perfect and true**
GRETA: THE WHOLE WORLD BECAME LIES!
EDNA: **I felt it when it hit me suddenly**
Hey, Harry?
ALL: **HA-A-ARRY**
EDNA: **Nobody loves you like m—**
ALL: **MEEEEEEEEEEEEEEE**

Sound of an elimination buzzer.

ALL: WHAT. THE. FAAAAH—

VERSE 3

LILY: **The judges said he was too young**
GRETA: **WHO EVEN ARE THEY?!**

DOM: **Tried to kick him off the show**

ASH: **WHY IS LIFE SO UNFAIYA?!**

SALTY: **But then they put him in a group**
With three more teenage boys
Who aren't as good as Harry

ALL BUT EDNA: **BUT THEY HAVE GREAT HAIR!**

Images of the world's biggest boy band, True Connection, are projected across the space.

SALTY: **Everybody said they couldn't last**
Thought as quick as they were manufactured
They would go backta maths class
They were boring, white bread—
They typecast them
But then their album was THE LITERAL BAST!

ASH: **Biggest debut that had even been seen**
Sold out malls turned into arenas
They sell perfumes, Listerine—

GRETA: **And UGG boots with HARRY'S FACE ON THEM!**

LILY: **If every fan of the band held hands it'd reach to Venus**

DOM: **Google gets forty million daily searches just for Harry's … hair!**

GRETA: **'Cause their music is actual, philosophical**
POETRYYYYYY

HARRY *appears on stage, lit like a god. He performs part of True Connection's hit song 'NOBODY' as the* FANS *sing along (with zero singing talent). They love him entirely. Across the space, we see videos of fans singing along in their bedrooms from all around the world (*VIDEO FAN CHORUS*).*

VERSE 4

HARRY & FANS: **I like your fingertips**
I like your soul
Thinking of your messy hair
I'm like woah
Forget the haters
Why they so mean?

Cause you're the biggest babe they've ever seen
Nothing's felt so real before
You got me scared to feel so sure
And I know every guy
Secretly wants you but ohh
Oh-oh Oh-oh-oh
Oh Oh-oh-oh
Nobody loves you, loves you like me
Nobody loves you, loves you like me
Nobody loves you, loves you like me
Girl nobody loves you, not like I do

HARRY *disappears. The pop track melts away and the* FANS' *singing becomes tender and vulnerable.*

An ocean of short sentences is projected across the space. We are swimming in fans' messages to Harry:

'did u get my letters?', 'love you baby', 'falling asleep thinking of u', 'plz notice me', 'love your smile', 'love ur pecks', 'luv u my cupcake', 'how was ur day', etc.

MELTING CHORUS

ALL: **Nobody loves you, loves you like me**
Nobody loves you, loves you like me
Nobody loves you, loves you like me
No, nobody loves you
Not like I do

VERSE 5

EDNA: **They just love you 'cause you're famous, but I don't care**
I see past the branding, I see past the … hair

I see a different person hiding in plain sight
And it makes me sound crazy, but I know that I'm right

'Cause I know how it feels to swallow a scream
While everyone tells you who you should be

But with you, I'm complete, and completely undone
I feel you take my hand, I hear you whisper … RUN!

BRIDGE

ALL: **You're on the backs of my eyelids**
The folds of my brain
You ruin my life
And you make my day

EDNA: **Because in your eyes I'm someone I wanna beeee**
Hey Harry!

BUILD-UP

ASH: **Hey Darling!**

SALTY: **Hey Husband!**

GRETA: **Hey Cupcake!**

DOM: **Hey Pumpkin!**

LILY: **Hey Pork Chop!**

ALL: **Nobody loves you like—**

ASH: **Hey Honey!**

GRETA: **Hey Dumpling!**

DOM: **Hey Daddy!**

EDNA: Hey HARRY!
Nobody looooooooooves y—

LILY *interrupts with an intimidating riff.*

LILY: **You-u-u-u-u-u-u-u-u**

EDNA: Like …

ALL: **MEEEEEEEEEEE**

Their gospel chord rises up into a squeal.

SCENE 4—P.E. CHANGE ROOMS—LUNCHTIME

BRIANNA *is showing* JULES *a video on her phone. They wear P.E. uniforms.* JULES *is in a foul mood.*

JULES: What a DUMB ATTENTION-SEEKING SLUT! WHAT is she doing-a?! GET UP, YOU COW!

BRIANNA: I would never faint on the stage. Like backstage I would, but not *on* the stage.

JULES: How does she even get to go up there?

BRIANNA: I heard she has cancer

JULES: Get UP, bitch! She's not even that hot.

EDNA *enters in normal uniform.*

EDNA: I thought we said tuckshop?

BRIANNA: [*to* EDNA] Have you seen the video of the / fainting girl?!

EDNA: Who faints onstage during 'Nobody'?

BRIANNA: Yeah!

EDNA: And Harry's face when he catches her?!

BRIANNA: / WHAT?!

EDNA: It's at two minutes seventeen seconds, wait—THERE! Pause it. / Oh my god!

BRIANNA: Oh my god, look, Jules! He's like a little pastry!

EDNA: No, look! At his eyes. This's what I've been talking about.

JULES: Oh my god, Harry is not depressed. You just wish he was.

EDNA: He literally IS. Can you even imagine having his life? Being supervised when you do literally anything other than go to the toilet? When I meet him, I'm seriously not even going to act like a fan. Like instead of asking for a hug, I'm just going to be like—do you need a hug?

JULES: Sorry … when are you meeting him?

EDNA: I just mean like, one day

JULES: 'Cause they're literally not even touring here, so.

BRIANNA: [*changing the subject*] Did you see Jules' new backpack?

BRIANNA *passes it to* EDNA. *It's got Harry's face on it.*

EDNA: Woah …

JULES: Mum's just trying to buy my love at the moment so I like her more than Dad. I could seriously make her do anything right now. Seriously.

EDNA: How are things at home?

JULES: FINE!

EDNA: … How's things with Jason?

JULES *freezes. Furious.*

BRIANNA: [*gesturing for* EDNA *to drop it*] He asked out Teagan.

JULES: I don't even care! TEAGAN has a moustache! Okay? She's not even hot!

BRIANNA: What moustache?

JULES: The one she gave herself when she tried to wax her upper lip with duct tape. Like an idiot.

BRIANNA: Do I have a moustache?

JULES: The ONLY reason he even asked her out is because she put up that pic. But just because you post a pic in only a pink bra does NOT mean that you are hot. It just means that you are THIRSTY!

BRIANNA: Are my pics thirsty?

JULES: No! Your pics are like—the opposite.

BRIANNA: Is that a good thing?

JULES: I just can't believe she stole him. I've been looking at him across the bus ALL year. I was GOING to talk to him.

BRIANNA: It'll be okay, Jules …

JULES: Will it? She's the seventh person in the year to get a boyfriend. We haven't even kissed anyone. None of the boys on the bus even look at us.

EDNA: Don't worry about them, Jules, the boys on the bus are gross anyway.

JULES: [*offended*] … What are you trying to say?

EDNA: Well. Like, they're a bit … immature?

JULES: You're immature.

EDNA: What?

JULES: You literally believe that you're gonna have Harry's babies.

BRIANNA: [*terrified*] Do you not love True Connection anymore?

JULES: I mean I love them, but there's a difference between being a fan of the band, and literally saving yourself for Harry. She thinks she's better than me 'cause I like real boys, but at least I'm not cray-zy.

EDNA: Well, I'd rather be … crazy … than be someone who's too chicken to even talk to boys on the bus.

JULES: I'M NOT A CHICKEN!

BRIANNA: / Guys, stop.

EDNA: You're chicken and you eat chicken corn.

BRIANNA: Guys!

JULES: Can I tell you something? As a friend, Edna? You are never. Going to be. With Harry. Harry is rich, and famous, and he dates models. Look at you, you're a fourteen-year-old fangirl and you write psycho fan fiction about him where you go on the run together and kill cops.

EDNA: WHAT? NO I DON'T!

JULES *gets out her phone and searches for a screenshot.*

JULES: Oh, really? So you didn't write about HARRY stabbing a cop in the stomach and then—wait for it—and then chucking—Here it is! 'With no time to lose, they lifted the officer's blood-soaked body into the bin.'

EDNA *battles* JULES *for the phone and begs her to stop, but* JULES *keeps reading*:

/ 'Then, Harry folded her into his arms—and for a second—time stood still.'

EDNA: Jules! Stop it!

JULES: 'Shhh,' he said, 'now the only real thing is us.' GET OFF ME IT'S MY PHONE!

The phone flies out of JULES *hands and crashes to the ground. Everyone holds their breath.* JULES *walks over to it. Checks if it's cracked. She sighs.*

I cannot BELIEVE you almost just BROKE my PHONE!
You're almost fifteen. It might be time to grow up.

JULES *leaves.*

EDNA: I asked you not to show her, Bri.

JULES: [*offstage*] BRIANNA!

BRIANNA *is torn. She wants to say something, but can't.*

BRIANNAAAA!

BRIANNA *goes.* EDNA *sings.*

SONG: 'WAIT AND SEE'

VERSE 1

EDNA: **On the fourth day of high school**
Heading home, all alone on the bus

I hadn't found any friends
A scholarship misfit swimming in rich kids
Till you turned and said
'Hey, come sit with us'

Suddenly, we were
Speaking in-a-language only we spoke
Giggling, non-stop
Laughing without even telling a joke

I remember sleeping over every single Saturday
Staying awake in a sweet sugar rush
There wasn't a secret that we couldn't trade
And there was nothing like us

Never thought I could hate you
Till you said it's time to 'grow up'
You say I'm crazy, 'cause I'm in love. Well,
It doesn't hurt because
Because …

CHORUS 1

I don't know when
I don't know how
But I know one day that
He'll look at me, and

He will love me then
Like I love him now
Just you wait … and see

POST-CHORUS 1

Oh, just you wait and see
Oh, just you wait
I'm not done becomin' who I'm gunna be.
Just you wait—

BRIDGE

You think I don't know him,
But I do, more than anyone
'Cause he used to be, just like me
A scholarship kid with a single mum

He's trying to do her proud, but he's a
Shy kid who hates these crowds

And I bet he
Wants a way out

And I know, we're on opposite sides
Of this rock
And each girl that he meets is a tick
On his clock

But what if I'm his tock?
I'm his 'ever after'?
And everything he never knew that he needed
Is what I've got?

CHORUS 2

I don't know when
I don't know how
But I know one day that
He'll look at me, and

He will love me then
Like I love him now
Just you wait … and see

POST-CHORUS 2

Oh, just you wait and see
Oh, just you wait
In one look, he'll realise I'm all that he needs
Just you wait
Oh, just you wait and see

EDNA *puts up two middle fingers.*

SCENE 5—EDNA'S KITCHEN—DINNERTIME

CAROLINE: EDDY, FOR THE LAST TIME!
EDNA: I'm here!

EDNA *arrives at the dinner table. She starts blowing on her soup restlessly.*

CAROLINE: Just wait for it to cool down, you silly bill.
How was school?

EDNA: Fine.

EDNA *tries a spoonful. Way too hot.*

CAROLINE: Just *wait*, teddy bear. What's the rush?

EDNA: I just have lots of homework so …

CAROLINE: Oh, is *that* why you were on your computer for six hours last night?

EDNA: … Yes?

CAROLINE: You sure you haven't just been googling what's his face?

EDNA: Mum!

CAROLINE: I know you think I'm old and annoying. But trust me, one day you'll thank me for trying to stop you from wasting your time on too much of that stuff.

EDNA: Mum-a!

CAROLINE: I know, your body is changing—and you want to project, certain feelings, but it's important to me that you understand that those boys are—

EDNA: Oh my god.

CAROLINE: Products designed to reinforce all of these toxic ideas about who you / are—

EDNA: Oh my GOD!

CAROLINE: It's just important to me that you know that they're artificial. Okay?

EDNA: Okay. Are you done?

CAROLINE: … Yes.

Pause.

EDNA *starts shovelling soup into her mouth.*

It's just that, it's … SO amazing that you've won this scholarship and I don't want you to waste this exciting opportunity over some, pop star.

EDNA *lifts the bowl and drains it.*

[*Disgusted*] Oh, Ed!

EDNA: Oh my god, Mum, you're literally telling me to do homework and that's all I'm trying to do. MAY I be excused?

CAROLINE: You didn't touch your bread.

EDNA: May I take my bread to my room and do my homework?

Beat.

CAROLINE: Okay. I love you, Ed—

EDNA*'s already gone.*

SCENE 6—FAN FIC FORUM

EDNA *opens her laptop.*

EDNA: Sorry I'm late! My mum is the most annoying person in the whole world. Did you read my 'on the run' story yet? What do you think?

LILY: I think it's sexy how they're on the run, but … I just don't think that Harry would kill a cop.

GRETA: Yeah.

EDNA: As if?! He totally would kill a cop if it was for *love*.

LILY: But not with a knife though!

GRETA: He wouldn't want them to feel pain.

LILY: He would *never.*

SALTY *appears. He's magical.*

SALTY: What if Harry made the cop inhale chloroform until they passed out?

EDNA: Go on @Saltypringl!

LILY: What's 'chloroform'?

SALTY: [*clapping on each word*] Clo. Ro. Form.

It's a chemical. You soak a rag in it and then you make people sniff it till they pass out.

DOM: But how would Harry get chloroform?

SALTY: You can literally google the recipe. Here:

He sends the link.

It's just nail polish remover, bleach and disinfectant.

Everyone's stunned.

EDNA: Wait, isn't it three a.m. in Utah?

SALTY: HOW AM I SUPPOSED TO EVER SLEEP AGAIN IN MY LIFE AFTER READING THAT FIC?

EDNA: Did you like it?

SALTY: Did I *like* it? I'm PREGNANT with it! You're like, the [Beyoncé] of fan fiction, seriously. Harry on the run from his evil management? IT'S ICONIC!

And I'm personally OBSESSED with the part where they kill the cop! Like I'm *actually* getting that whole paragraph tattooed on my face. Like I'll never get a job now because it's going to be tattooed on my face. Forever.

LILY: I just don't believe that Harry would be that cruel—

All the FANS *speak at once, a cacophony of notes*: *'Yeah and I dunno about the part where ...' 'What if instead they ...' 'I just have one suggestion ...'*

SALTY *clicks—the* FANS *freeze.*

SALTY: Ignore them. It's literally the best thing I've ever read.

EDNA: Thanks, Salty. I had the worst day, so.

Suddenly, we're in a private chat between EDNA *and* SALTY. *The way they talk to each other is more relaxed and familiar.*

SALTY: Talk to me.

EDNA: Just. Mum keeps telling me Harry is literally ruining my life. Oh, and today I got called crazy for writing fan fiction, oh, AND I don't really have any friends anymore, so …

SALTY: Excuse me?

EDNA: I mean *school* friends.

SALTY: Well, I'm sorry to hear your *school* friends are trash. How can I help?

EDNA: Distract me?

SALTY: Oh … you mean with my. Fresh. [*Pose.*] New. [*Pose.*] Fic?

Pose, pose, pose.

For each pose we hear a drum hit.

EDNA: You wrote a new story?

SALTY: I mean it's just a draft but …

Fasten your seatbelt …

Boom!

Pack yourself a SNACK …

Boom!

Because I'm about to take you … on a JOURNEY.

Boom boom boom!

SALTY *sings to* EDNA. *The* FANS *sing backup.*

SONG: 'FEELS SO TRUE'

VERSE 1

SALTY: **He's not in the band,**
He's new at your school
Rugby captain, always trapped in
Between tryhards and tools
It's lunchtime, and your lonely
Sandwich clutched to your chest
You'll eat it in the library,
Cause all your friends … are books

You cut behind the science block, turn the corner,
And. He's. There.
He picks your sandwich up
Then he flicks his perfect hair

He asks for a minute
He gets the rest of your day
And he tells you
What he's been dying to say

FANS: **He tells youuuuuu**

CHORUS 1

SALTY: **When this world**
Is messy and cruel
I build one that's better
I go there with you

Where we can be
Anyone we wanna be
Feels more real than reality
Don't care if it's a daydream
Baby, it feels so
True

The ensemble hand SALTY *two machine guns. He hands one to* EDNA.

SALTY: [*to* EDNA] New vibe. You'll need this.

VERSE 2

SALTY: **Stuck in the bunker**
Ever since the attack
When your mum left to get food
She became a zombie snack

So now your only family
Is a British boy
His hair is like summer
His eyes are like the truth

EDNA: **Just friends, but there is something more**
Between you that you can't ignore

LILY: Are you long-lost twins?

SALTY: What the hell? No!
You're just two boys
Who've never felt so alive
Than in each other's arms
So you better survive—

ALL: **The zoooooombies!**
Die, bitch, die!

Sound of a machine gun firing. Splat! Splat!

CHORUS 2

ALL: **When this world**
Is messy and cruel
I build one that's better
I go there with you

Where we can be
Anyone we wanna be
Feels more real than reality
Don't care if it's a daydream
Baby, it feels so
True

BRIDGE

SALTY: **There's a me I'm scared to be**
There's words I'd never say out loud
But when I'm with you
Anything is allowed

EDNA: **Because you switch off the bitches**
You wipe their words away
Delete it all, I can feel it
I finally feel okay

SALTY: **Magnificent things**
Are always misunderstood
Who's to say this is no good
Right here I feel myself mending

EDNA: **And if it's all just pretend**
Why is this the only place
Where I'm not

ALL: **Pretending?**

LILY: **WOAHHHHHHHHHHHHH**

An amazing riff.

CHORUS 3

ALL: **When this world**
Is messy and cruel
I build one that's better
I go there with you

Where we can be
Anyone we wanna be
Feels more real than reality
Don't care if it's a daydream
Baby, it feels so—

The arrangement slows.

SALTY: [*heartfelt*] **This world**
Is messy and cruel
So when you need one that's better
I'll build it for you

Where you can be
Anyone you wanna be
'Cause I know you'd do the same for me
So let them call you crazy
But I believe in you

SALTY *shoots one last zombie. Splat.*

EDNA: Hey, thanks for cheering me up.

SALTY: Anytime. Okay, I should probs do sleeping.

EDNA: Hey—is it a bit, psycho? My story? The stabbing part?

SALTY: What? No. It's la-hiterally incredible. Plus everyone is going to go crazy for it now that Helsinki's happened. Sweet dreams!

He goes to leave.

EDNA: Wait what? What happened in Helsinki?

SALTY: The trash can … in Harry's hotel room?

EDNA: What are you talking about?

SALTY: Some fans broke into his hotel room in Helsinki and found an empty sheet of antidepressants in the trash. Here's the link.

Whoosh.

EDNA: So Harry IS depressed?

SALTY: Totally! Some fans are saying he's been in therapy since February—because his management won't let him leave the band!

EDNA: But that's exactly—

SALTY: Literally what your fic was about. It's like / Psychic.

EDNA: Destiny.

SALTY: I just can't believe his management are doing this to him! But I also can because we ALL know that they are covering up multiple gay relationships in the band.

EDNA: Hey, Salty, would ever consider like, co-writing a story? With someone? Like, maybe me?

SALTY: Are you kidding?! That would complete my entire existence!

EDNA: What if we wrote a prologue? To my on-the-run fic? Which could tell the story of *how* this fourteen-year-old fan found a way to actually reach Harry. And how she convinced him to leave the band, and go on the run with her.

SALTY: OH MY GOD, and it can expose how much his management are total DICKS!

EDNA: Exactly, but it can also explain how she makes direct contact with him. Would you be down to, do some research? Help me think of some ideas?

SALTY: UM? Is half the band in the closet? YES! OBVIOUSLY YES! ONE HUNJI PERCENT! YES! Let's start tomorrow!

EDNA: Sweet dreams, Salty.

SALTY: Sweet dreams, friend.

SONG: 'SET YOU FREE'

EDNA *sings with shock and determination.*

EDNA: **I knew I saw it in his eyes**
I knew I wasn't crazy, I knew that I was right
I saw the secret hell he's living in

I don't know where
I don't know how
But I just know that
We're going to meet

He'll see I'm the one
Take my hand and run
When I set
Him free

FANS: **Ha-a-a-rry**

EDNA: **How do I set you free?**

The track ends like a lullaby. EDNA *sleeps.*

SCENE 7—THE ANNOUNCEMENT

JULES *is asleep under a Harry bedspread. A True Connection song plays out of her phone ('Cool Girl'). She swats off her alarm and grabs her phone.*

The track soars into clarity. BRIANNA, *in a True Connection nightie, shaving her moustache. She mumble-sings along to the track.*

On the beat, EDNA *gets ready for school. Sniffs her armpits. Her cheap phone buzzes. She unlocks it and then:*

The track cuts. FANS *across the space stare at their phones.* EDNA *reads her screen, shocked.*

EDNA: Morning, beautiful …
I hope you dreamed sweetly …
I have a surprise for you …
TrueConnection.com?!

Everyone clicks the link. Gasps. We see the video they're watching.

HARRY: Hi. I'm Harry from True Connection …
(We've got a) bit of surprise for our beautiful Aussie fans …
We've added last-minute tour dates …
Tickets on sale tomorrow at ten a.m.
We can't wait to finally meet you.
[*Reverby*] Meet you—meet you—meet you.

ALL: Whaaaaaaaaa!

BRIANNA and JULES: [*together, blood-curdling*] MUUUUUM!

EDNA: [*breathless*] Harry!

LILY *appears in a video projected in the space. She's on her vlog.*

SONG: 'ACTUALLY DEAD'

INTRO

LILY: **Harry, I'm dying**
This news just ended my life
I'm thirteen, whatcha mean—the CHEAPEST seats are ONE THIRTY-NINE NINETY-FIVE?

Seriously
I am talking to you, HAROLD
This is your wife speaking
Reply to my tweets and explain yourself
After all I've done for you, HARRY, you go and kill my life!
What the HELL thirteen-year-old has ONE THIRTY-NINE NINETY-FIVE?

ROSA, RIWA, JULES, *and* BRIANNA *appear in school uniform.*

CHORUS 1

ALL: **Thi-hi-his is life or death**

I can't even! What is breath?
If I don't go then
I-I-I'll be AC-TU-A-LLY dead

They death drop. EDNA *enters, pursuing* CAROLINE.

CAROLINE: Leave it, Eddy.

EDNA: Mum, I never ask for anything

CAROLINE: I know this feels like it's life-threatening, but trust me, when you're a bit older you'll see that—

EDNA: You're not LISTENING!

FAN VERSE

ROSA: **What do you mean tickets go on sale tomorrow?**
AT TEN A.M?
That's during school, Harry! Fire your manager!
That literally makes NO sense

RIWA: **Harry, excuse me, baby**
Why are you being so racist?
You can't tour Australia
And just skip Tasmania
That's literally like placist!

They death drop again. JULES *and* BRIANNA *at school. Lunchtime.*

BRIANNA: My mum said no.

JULES: WHAT!

BRIANNA: She said I already spent my birthday money.

JULES: Then ask for early Christmas money?!

BRIANNA: I already spent that on Harry's new perfume …

JULES: Ask your dad. He takes your brother to the football every weekend.

BRIANNA: He said it's different.

JULES: Bri! I can't just stand in the mosh pit with my loser mum like a BISCUIT!

EDNA *enters, upset.*

BRIANNA: Eddy! Are you going?

EDNA: No. My MUM'S a BITCH!

BRIANNA & JULES: Woah …

PRETZEL VERSE

EDNA: **That. Cow. Said. To Me.**

CAROLINE *appears for this verse.*

EDNA & CAROLINE: **Edna, society twists girls when they hit puberty**
Into petrified pretzels of insecurity
So when four boys with hair that sits perfectly
Promise in their songs to love you in perpetuity
It's just a product, a packaged preteen fantasy
So your love is not reality 'cause he's a celebrity
You're just projecting onto
An infallible effigy

BRIANNA: What the eff's an effigy?

EDNA: Um, an effigy is like a model or representation of a / pers—

JULES: Your mum's weird.

BRIANNA: Well, at least you and I can just have a sleepover that night and sing all their songs while we cry ourselves to sleep.

JULES: YOU'RE NOT HAVING A SLEEPOVER!

I mean … because you're coming. You have to. It's what we've always dreamed of.

BRIANNA: But tickets go on sale at ten a.m. tomorrow.

EDNA: They'll sell out in seconds.

JULES: Yeah, we know. Come on, Edna, you're on a full scholarship. Surely that brain can think of something?

I can't just go with my MUM!

Something takes over EDNA. *Dark underscoring.*

EDNA: Then why don't *you* buy our tickets, Jules?

JULES: What? I don't have that money …

EDNA: But your mum does. And you said she's buying your love at the moment. You said you could make her do anything. Remember?

JULES: Yeah but—

EDNA: Unless you're a …

Chicken.

Everyone gasps. Including ROSA *and* RIWA.

JULES *get out her phone and dials. Everyone holds their breath.*

THE PHONE CALL

JULES:
Hey, Mummy, how are you?
Yes I do. Sometimes. Call you that
Well, I know you're probably busy
But I'm having a panic attack
You know that ticket that you're getting
I need you to get more
BECAUSE! I can't go alone with you
And my friends are totally poor
If you get them my mental health stays intact
If you don't I'll get depressed cripplingly sad
Therapy's expensive—I don't that think you'd want that—

ROSA, RIWA, BRIANNA & EDNA:
Ooooohhhh
Ooooohhhh
Ooooohhhh
Mmmmmmmmm
Mummy, Mummy, Mummy,
Mummy, Mummy, Mummy,
Mummy, Mummy, Mummy,
Mummy, Mummy, Mummy,
Mummy, Mummy, Mummy
SO POOOOOR
INTAAAACT
SUPER FAAAAT
AHHHHHH!

JULES: Mum, if I don't go *I'll die*—I'M NOT BEING OVERDRAMATIC. Mum?!

EDNA: Come on, Jules!

JULES: **If you don't get these tickets**
I don't know what I'll do
I might have to send Dad
the photos of you
That I found on your phone
In a message to—

ALL BUT JULES: [*anxious, melodramatic harmonies*]
Aaaaah …

JULES: Yeah, so that's mosh pit—Tuesday the twelfth.
You'll get them tomorrow. You promise? Like actually?
Ohmygod. Thanks Mummy loveyoubye!

EDNA: Jules?

JULES: Oh my god.
BRIANNA: Oh. My. GOD!

PRE-CHORUS

BRIANNA: **Google my symptoms, I think I'm dead**
JULES: **Plan my funeral, 'cause I think I'm DEAD**
EDNA: **Identify my body, 'cause I think I'm DEAD**
BRIANNA: **This news is like a brick to the FACE!**

CHORUS 2

ALL: **OH MY GOD, I'M ACTUALLY DEAD!**
I can't even! What is breath?
JULES: MY UTERUS IS EXPLODING!
ALL: **IIII'm ACTUALLY dead**
BRIANNA: **Hold me, I can see a bright light!**
JULES: **Get a coffin and chuck me inside!**
EDNA: **It's the best day of my life!**
ALL: **'Cause IIIIII'm. ACTUALLY DEAD!**

ROSA, RIWA, JULES *and* BRIANNA *disappear.*

SCENE 8—GOT NO CHILL

EDNA *quakes with the realisation that she's going to the concert.*

SONG: 'GOT NO CHILL'

INTRO

EDNA: **I knew I was meant to save you**
Now I know how I will
The chances you don't take
Are the monsters you make
This is my one chance
So I've got. No. Chill.

Epic battle drums. SALTY *appears.*

EDNA: SALTY. I've had a brainwave. About the story we're working on?
SALTY: MY BODY IS READY!

VERSE 1

EDNA: **Our protagonist, I've been thinking**
How could she track him down?
She can't book a flight if she's fourteen, so
That doesn't work, BUT!

What if Harry played a concert
In her hometown?
What if that's where they meet?!
What if he comes to HER?!

SALTY: LOLLLL, how would she ever meet him at a concert?

EDNA: **There has to be some way that she can catch his eye**
Some way to show him that she knows
He's only half alive
That he's trapped inside his own life

SALTY: But HOW-A?

EDNA: **Um … Maybe. She could. Make a. Sign?**

The track cuts.

SALTY: A SIGN?! Are you drunk? There's a tens of thousands people at their concerts.

EDNA: But what if she like, found him somehow and like, talked to him privately / and—

SALTY: *WHAT?!* Where is she going to do that? In his toilet? When he does a poop? Babe, you know that Harry is supervised 24/7. There's NO way they could EVER meet at a concert.

EDNA: Or is that just what management WANT us to think?

SALTY: Nnnnno, babe. There's LA-HITERALLY no way that—

SALTY *has a revelation. Awestruck.*

OH … MY … GOD …

EDNA: What?

SALTY: Oh. My. God.

EDNA: What?

SALTY: Unless …

EDNA: WHAT?!

SALTY: Cancer!

EDNA: … Salty?

Underscore: *tense strings.*

SALTY: The boys always sing to a girl with cancer.

EDNA: But she doesn't have …

SALTY: AND IT'S SUPER UNFAIR, BECAUSE THEY NEVER PICK *BOYS* WITH CANCER. OR *BOYS* AT ALL, EVER!

But, assuming your protagonist is a girl—why doesn't she just … pretend to be sick?

EDNA: What?

SALTY: And when Harry sings to her / on stage—

EDNA: She could pass him a NOTE! About how they need to run away together—

SALTY: Wait, you're right—this is WAYYYY better!

EDNA: But, would that actually work? How would she even look like—

SALTY: Oh, get READY, gurl.

Backup DANCERS *join* SALTY. *He is Britney.*

VERSE 2

SALTY: **She just needs to SHAVE. HER. HEAD!**

EDNA: What?

SALTY: **She just needs to LOOK LIKE SHE'S ALMOST DEAD.**

EDNA: Wait, but …

SALTY: **It'll all be worth the price**
When she gets on stage and he looks in her eyes

EDNA: **And she slips him a note telling him that only she knows**

SALTY & EDNA: **Everything that he's trying to hide!**

ENSEMBLE: **A NOTE!**

SALTY: **It'll say she knows he's depressed**

ENSEMBLE & EDNA: **DEPRESSED!**

SALTY: **But tonight's his chance to restart**

ENSEMBLE & EDNA: **RESTART!**

SALTY: **It'll say the number plate of the getaway car**
Waiting in the car park

EDNA: But how would she like steal a car? Let alone learn to drive?

SALTY: Internet? Duh!

EDNA: Oh my god, you're right.

Underscore: *dramatic, tense strings.*

But if she shaves her head … will Harry still think she's pretty?

SALTY: Of course he will! When she explains why she did it, he'll be so grateful. Besides. It'll grow back when they're on the run.

EDNA: You're right … he'd understand.

SALTY: I'm obsessed with how dark this is. Can you imagine if someone actually did this?

EDNA: Yeah … imagine …

SALTY'S DANCERS *tear away* EDNA*'s uniform to reveal her dream outfit. Suddenly, we are at True Connection's concert in* EDNA*'s fantasy.*

VERSE 3

EDNA: **Security walks me to the side of the stage**
Past the barriers, the arms reaching through like a cage
Climb the stairs, lights glaring down
In a tight square
I'm standing right there
Screams blaring
Ninety thousand eyeballs staring
Focus, pretend they're not there
And suddenly the searing screams stop

HARRY *appears. Staring at her.*

You turn and see me, you just stare
It's like you've met me

EDNA & HARRY: **Can't think where …**

EDNA: **In just one look, you'll realise**

EDNA:	HARRY:
Without me you've only	**Without you I've only**
Been half alive	**Been half alive**
That only I	
Can set you free	**Can set me free**
Because in my eyes	
You're someone you wanna be	**I'm someone I wanna be**

HARRY *sings a capella and walks towards her.*

HARRY: **Let them all say we're wrong**
Let's leave them in our dust
'Cause now the only real

Inches from her face. He does a long sexy riff and stares into her eyes.

Thi-i-i-ing. Is us.

HARRY *disappears. The beat returns.*

VERSE 4

EDNA: **You do the choreography, you give me a hug**
But you don't want to let me out of your arms
As you sing the chorus, you take my hand
And that's when I'll slip the note in your palm

Why should we live as others decide?
In hiding we'll finally have nothing to hide

Just you and me
A backpack of cash and our fake IDs
Just you and me
A backpack of cash and our fake IDs!

The backup DANCERS *re-appear in unbelievable outfits.* EDNA *considers her plan. A new confidence washes over her. Her eyes become wild with determination.*

The DANCERS *sing* EDNA*'s words back to her. The layers build.*

BUILD-UP

LAYER 1: **You and me, a backpack of cash and our fake IDs**
LAYER 2: **The chances you don't take are the monsters you make**
LAYER 3: **Just you wait and seeee**
LAYER 4: **Just usssss**

EDNA *sings over them, in a trance.*

EDNA: **Let them all say we're wrong, let's leave them in our dust**
'Cause now the only real thing is us

This world is messy and cruel
I'll build one that's better
I'll build it for you

The beat drops. They dance. EDNA *is possessed. Nothing can stop her now.*

EDNA: **Hey Harryyyyyy**
Hey Harryyyyyy
Hey Harryyyyyy
Hey Harryyyyyy

DANCERS: [*layered harmonies*]
Nobody loves you, loves you like me. [*repeating*]

EDNA: **Nobody loves you, loves you like me**

Huge explosive drum hit.

SCENE 9—SCHOOL—LUNCHTIME

JULES *and* BRIANNA *at school.*

JULES: WHAT THE ACTUAL LITERAL HELL?! Amelia Gottleib? As if SHE'S got a boyfriend.
BRIANNA: They've only been out one time though. And they kissed but I don't know if it was even with tongues.
JULES: She's the NINTH person in the year to get a boyfriend, Bri! We're going to be the last ones and then we're going to be emotionally deformed for the rest of our lives. What the HELL?! Amelia Gottleib literally isn't even hot. Everyone just THINKS she is because of her pics, but she always crops out her weird knees
BRIANNA: What's wrong with her knees?
JULES: You've seen them! They're gross!

BRIANNA *looks down at her own knees in horror.* EDNA *runs on.*

EDNA: SURPRISE!

She thrusts a Tupperware to JULES.

BRIANNA: Ohmygod, what's in there?!
EDNA: KIT. KAT. COOKIES! [*To* JULES] Your favourite!
BRIANNA: OH MY GOD! WE HAVEN'T HAD THEM IN AGES! REMEMBER THAT SLEEPOVER WE ATE TWO TRAYS OF THEM IN LIKE EIGHT MINUTES!
JULES: Lol, when I ate gluten.

She gives the Tupperware back.

EDNA: Oh. Sorry. I didn't know.
But I'll just … make them again. Without gluten. 'Cause I, I just really want to thank you. Jules.
'Causc this is probably going to be the best night of our lives.

BRIANNA: OH MY GOD, WHAT ARE WE GUNNA WEAR?!

EDNA: Right?! But first, I want to talk to you both about *safety*. 'Cause I've thought about it and we should definitely make sure that we each have our OWN copy of the tickets on the night—just in case we split up—

BRIANNA: But why would we split up? We're going to be together the whole time. Three friends. Together. Being friends.

EDNA: I mean in case we *got* split up. By accident. Like, better safe than sorry, right? So, Jules, it would be great if you could forward us the email with the tickets? For safety? Is that cool?

JULES *looks away.*

JULES: Yeah, about that.

BRIANNA: What?

JULES *shrugs.*

EDNA: You … got the tickets … right?

JULES: Of course I got tickets. Mum got them today.

EDNA *and* BRIANNA *explode with relief.*

EDNA: Then what?

JULES: Nothing.

BRIANNA: Ohmygod! Jules-A!

EDNA: Ohmygod, that scared me!

JULES: But she. She could only get one more so.

A terrible silence.

EDNA: *One* more?

JULES: Well like, one for her, and one for me and … one more.

BRIANNA: What? Why?

JULES: [*lying*] She just … couldn't.

EDNA: … So. … so who's …?

JULES: Sorry, Edna, It's for Bri.

EDNA *is devastated.* JULES *tries to hide her guilt.*

Look, far out. I just. Mum said it's for you, Bri.

EDNA: As if she did.

JULES: [*lying*] … She did.

EDNA: No she. Jules, what? How am I gunna go now? I have to go!

JULES: Get a ticket off eBay.
EDNA: For a thousand bucks?
JULES: Look, I'm sorry.
EDNA: Bri, are you going?
BRIANNA: Well—
JULES: Yes. You are. I got you a ticket.
BRIANNA: Um …
JULES: Bri. Don't be mean to my mum.
BRIANNA: Why don't we … make it up to you, Ed? We could all—

EDNA *runs off before they can see her cry.*

Eddy!

SCENE 10—DON'T EXIST

A cacophony of whispers rises up. The space is flooded with videos of the same FANS *we saw earlier (the* VIDEO FAN CHORUS*). They each stare into their phone or laptop camera, as if they're recording a message just for Harry.* EDNA *appears on stage, and breaks into pieces.*

SONG: 'DON'T EXIST'

INTRO

FANS: **Hey Harry**
FAN 1: I just wanted to tell you I love the new hairstyle—
FANS: **Hey Harry**
FAN 2: Hey Harry, I just did my English project about you, can I send it to you?—
FANS: **Hey Harry**
FAN 3: Hey Harry, I missed out on concert tickets, but while you're in town maybe you could come to my house for dinner? Mum says it's okay—

VERSE 1

FANS: **Hey Harry**
SALTY: **How was your day?**
FANS: **Hey Harry**
ASH: **Gymnastics was fun!**

FANS: **Hey Harry**

LILY: **Guess what?**
Today, for the first time,
Dad hit Mum

CHORUS 1

FANS: **Hey Harry**

LILY: **Hey Harry, put on your boxing gloves**
Aim for the head, don't miss
Knock my teeth out, babe, it'll hurt much less
Than you never knowing I ex—

JULES *and* BRIANNA *appear again.*

JULES: I can't believe it's only two weeks till we see the boys! Do you dare me to flash my tits at them?

BRIANNA: [*seeing* EDNA] Jules!

JULES: Ohmygod, I'm actually going to. But you HAVE to be ready to take a picture of Harry's face when he sees my tits.
I seriously wanna remember this night till I'm like, thirty!

EDNA *hurts more.*

VERSE 2

SALTY: **Got your selfies on my camera roll**
So I can pretend you stole my phone
I drew you pictures, did you get my letters?
About what's really going on at home

I hate to be a burden
I know how busy you are
I can see your life's perfect, like I'll never be
And baby, that thought leaves a scar

CHORUS 2

FANS: **Use my guts as your spaghetti**
Put your fork in and twist
Use my blood for your sauce
It'll hurt much less
Than you never knowing
I ex—

CAROLINE *appears.*

VERSE 3

CAROLINE: **Hey, Eddy**
Are you / okay?
EDNA: **I SAID GO AWAY**
CAROLINE: **Hey, Eddy**
Can we just / talk?
EDNA: **Just give me some space**
CAROLINE: **For weeks you haven't been yourself—why won't you just tell me what's wrong?**

EDNA: Why? So you can tell me it doesn't matter? And that I should focus on 'fulfilling my potential'?

CAROLINE: Is this about the concert?

EDNA: Why did you have me?

CAROLINE: What?

EDNA: If you couldn't afford it. Then why did you? We never have anything. Our place is tiny and I hate this ugly backpack I've had since Year Five and I hate the ugly RUG and I don't have any space and you never *give* me any space you just always barge in and—

CAROLINE: I chose to have you because I love you, Edna.
I'm sorry if you don't feel like I give you. Anything.

EDNA *leaves.*

BRIDGE

ALL: **You're on the backs of my eyelids**
The folds of my brain
You ruin my life
And you make my day
CAROLINE: **But in your eyes**
I'm not who you want me to be
Oh, Eddy
Eddy
Nobody loves you like. Meeeee

BREAKDOWN

CAROLINE *and the* FANS *sing. Heartbroken.*

CAROLINE: **If I don't exist, I don't exist to you**
Well then, do I exist? Do I exist at all? [*Repeating*]
FANS GROUP 1: **If I don't exist, I don't exist to you**
Well then, do I exist? Do I exist at all? [*Repeating*]
FANS GROUP 2: **Never, never, never**
What if you never learn my name? [*Repeating*]
FANS GROUP 3: **Hey Harry. Hey Harry** [*Repeating*]

CAROLINE *leaves.* EDNA *appears. She holds a coil of rope. Suicidal.*

EDNA: **If I don't show you**
You won't know what you've missed
It'll hurt
But, it'll hurt much less
Than you never knowing I … exist.

SCENE 11—JULES' BEDROOM

Big sexy drums. JULES *and* BRIANNA *are getting ready for the concert. They're dressed comically try-hard.*

SONG: 'NIGHT OF OUR LIVES'

INTRO

JULES: New skirt!
BRIANNA: [*struggling to walk*] New shoes!
JULES: G-string I stole from Mum!
BRIANNA: Flower crown!
JULES: No, Brianna!

CHORUS 1

BRIANNA & JULES: **Tonight's gunna be the best night of our lives**
The 'everything changes' night of our lives
The most important night of our lives
Yeah, tonight's gunna be the best
JULES: NIGHT OF OUR LIVES, BITCH!

VERSE 1

JULES *stuffs her bra while* BRIANNA*'s in her own world.*

BRIANNA: **Fifteen weeks picking what to wear**
Planned my makeup and practised my hair
MADE this crown, bought a special glue
The wire cuts my scalp, but
BEAUTY IS PAIN!

It's worth it for the pics I'm gunna take tonight
It's worth it for the way they're gunna change my life
'Cause when I post these pics everyone will be like:
'WOAH. WAIT … Brianna isn't that ugly.'

CHORUS 2

BRIANNA: **Tonight's gunna be the best night of my life**
The 'Wow, Bri's actually gorgeous' night of my life
'Wow, Bri's not that flat' night of my life
'Bri could actually be a model'
Night of my life, bitch!

VERSE 2

JULES: **I'm dressing for the boys who aren't in the band**
BRIANNA: I don't think they have any straight male fans?
JULES: **Not the fans! Think of the girls who are ten**
Who they gunna drag along to chaperone them?
Hot big brothers!
Hot big brothers!
I'll sniff 'em out, push past the DRUNK MOTHERS
And I be like, 'Yo, this show is so lame'
He's like, 'Yeah, woah, I know right, same'
But in that skirt you look so hot it's insane
BRIANNA: But won't your mum be right there?
JULES: **Then he'll. Ask me. On A. Date**
Then I'll. Be like. Okay. Babe.
Then I. Kiss him. On the. Face!
Maybe. Go to. Second base—
—ase—aaaaase!

BRIANNA *gets distracted by her phone.*

CHORUS 3

JULES: **Tonight's gunna be the best night of my life**
The night everyone talks about night of my life
'Wow, Jules is such a slut!' night of my life
'I'm so jealous of her!' night of my life, B—

STOP IT!

BRIANNA?

BRIANNA: What?

JULES: Why are you being weird?

BRIANNA: I just. I feel a bit bad.

JULES: … It's not our fault.

BRIANNA: But. Jules. Edna like REALLY loves Harry.

JULES: Remember how my mum said that, like, she couldn't stay with my dad because he didn't 'elevate' her?

Well, that's like us, Bri. Edna was holding us back.

This is a really important time in our lives. If we stuck around with her, we'd probably graduate without EVER having had a boyfriend. And then we'd spend our ENTIRE lives regretting that we NEVER got to experience the most important part of being a teenager: Young. Love.

Beat.

I changed my mind. Let's drink the Red Bulls now.

JULES *produces two Red Bulls.*

BRIANNA: It's just … last time I had it it made me a bit seizure-y.

JULES: Brianna. There will never be another night like tonight. We're never going to be this young or hot or happy ever again in our WHOLE LIVES.

BRIANNA: You think I look hot?

JULES: Yeah … Heaps.

BRIANNA *opens a can. Crack. The lights go wild as the girls chug three Red Bulls each. The track becomes more and more hyper.* JULES *becomes utterly fierce.* BRIANNA *just becomes unhinged.*

JULES & BRIANNA: WE. LOOK. SO. HOT!

VERSE 3

JULES: **You're basic, I'm acid, I'm vinegar, I'm balsamic**
Call a therapist, I'm devastating, I'm traumatic
Call your mum like, 'Why can't I be that fierce?'
Use your fugly ugg boots to dry your tears

Sorry! It just occurred to me, as a courtesy
I should warn you, just got you all sick with jealousy
First symptom—is being obSESSed with me
Second symptom is ANAL BLEEDING!

BRIANNA: **Me and my com … erade**
We're the squad you wish you had
You wanna be like us so you feel really bad
And then you cry like ohmaGAD! ohmaGAD! ohmaGAD! ohmaGAD! ERMERGADDDDD!
SUCK A RED MAXI PAD!

The track cuts. BRIANNA *pants.*

JULES: Bri? … Bri? … Are you okay?

BRIANNA *burps.*

BRIANNA: … I've never felt BETTERRRRR.

CHORUS 4

JULES & BRIANNA: **Tonight's gunna be the best night of our lives**
The 'everything changes' night of our lives
The most important night of our lives
Yeah, tonight's gunna be the best
Night of our lives, BITCH!

BRIANNA: **Ohmygod,**
we look so hot
OHMYGOD! OHMYGOD!
OHMYGOD!

JULES: **Hot big brothers**
HOT BIG BROTHERS

JULES & BRIANNA: **The most important night of our lives**
Yeah, tonight's gunna be the best
NIGHT OF OUR LIVES, BITCH!

SCENE 12—EDNA'S BEDROOM—NIGHT OF THE CONCERT

EDNA *hears a knock on the door and hides the rope she's knotting.* CAROLINE *stays outside.*

EDNA: Yes?

CAROLINE: Do you want, there's dinner?

EDNA: No. Thank you. I will later.

CAROLINE: Okay. I don't have to go in until nine-thirty, so. I'll be around till then.

Beat.

And I know what tonight is, so I got ice-cream.

EDNA: Okay.

CAROLINE: Okay. I love you, Eddy.

EDNA *almost replies, when*:

Look, Eddy, I know you're angry at me because it feels like this is life or death. But I promise you, one day you'll realise that this isn't going to change your life—

EDNA *sings internally, missing the rest of this and drowning it out*:

PRE-CHORUS

EDNA: **Say WHAT you want** **You've GOT no clue** **Just how sorry, you're all gunna be** **When I am gone** **From your tiny world** **Just you wait** **And seeeeeee**	CAROLINE: I know it feels like these boys are everything, but I promise you that there are more important and wonderful things in this life. And it's just, it's dangerous that young women are taught that romantic love is the only end goal, because you are already so powerful in your own right, okay, Eddy? And I love you.

JULES, BRIANNA *and the rest of the* ENSEMBLE *arrive at the concert, hyper.*

CHORUS 5

EDNA:	ENSEMBLE:	BRIANNA & JULES:
Wait and see	**Nobody loves you loves you like me**	**Thi-hi-his is life or death! I can't even, what is breath?!**
Wait and see	**Nobody loves you loves you like me**	**I-I-I-I-I-I'm actually DEAD Tonight's gunna be the best night of our lives**
Wait and SEEEEEE	**Nobody loves you loves you like me**	**The everything changes night of our lives The most important night of our lives**
	Girl, nobody loves you, Not like—	**Yeah, tonight's gunna be the best**
		NIGHT OF OUR LIVES, BITCH!

SCENE 13—THE CONCERT

Suddenly, the concert is starting. Blinding light.

Drum drum.

A stadium of fans scream.

Drum drum.

The fans scream again.

Flash to: HARRY *holds his guitar in the air.*

HARRY: Good night [SYDNEY]!

The crowd goes wild. A sickening tinnitus sound. BRIANNA *and* JULES *stumble out of the concert, sobbing.*

BRIANNA: I can't believe my phone died. Where's my flower crown?

JULES: DID YOU SEE HIM LOOK AT ME? HARRY DEFINITELY LOOKED AT ME. I'm. Actually. So. DEADDDDDDD.

Blackout.

SCENE 14—EDNA'S BEDROOM—3.42 A.M.

Pitch black. A tight light reveals only the railing of Edna's wardrobe. A rope, knotted to it, is groaning. We can faintly see a figure in the wardrobe, with a pillowcase over their head.

The figure gasps a breath. A hand reaches out of the darkness to pull away the pillowcase. And that's when we realise. The figure isn't Edna, it's HARRY.

He is tied up, gagged and blindfolded in her wardrobe.

She's staring at him, dressed in black pants and a hoodie that reads 'CREW'.

HARRY *wriggles and lets out a gagged cry for help.* EDNA *claps a chloroform rag to his face. Just as he's about to go limp:*

Blackout.

INTERVAL

ACT TWO

AS THE AUDIENCE RETURN—STADIUM

*We have jumped back in time. We're at the stadium, but the concert has yet to start. Two hyper fans (*YAEL *and* GEORGIA*) make their way through the foyer / auditorium. They interact with the audience, saying stuff like:*

'Lol sorry. Sorry. Sorry. I'm just like down the row, so.'

'What the hell? I love your outfit! Where did you get those shoes?!'

'Anyone got some lip balm?'

'What do you think they're all doing right now? Backstage?'

They make friends, take selfies, start a standing wave, and lead the audience in a chant: 'We want Harry! We want Harry!'—when finally, it begins.

SCENE 1—THE CONCERT

Just like before: a blinding light.

Drum drum.

Fans scream.

Drum drum.

Fans scream again.

But this time, we don't fast forward: we see True Connection perform. HARRY *is the clear star. It's impossible not to love him.* YAEL *and* GEORGIA *react throughout.*

A pop guitar hook. The band spill onto the stage. The crowd goes wild. HARRY, ZAK, LEO, REES *and* MYLES *hype up the crowd, blowing kisses to various fans.*

'[Sydney]! Let me hear you!' 'Put your hands up!' 'I see you there, in the sweater!'

SONG: 'NOBODY'

HARRY: **I like your fingertips, I like your soul**
Thinking of your messy hair, I'm like woah
Forget the haters, why they so mean?
'Cause you're the biggest babe they've ever seen

REES: *Here we go!*

HARRY:	REST OF TRUE CONNECTION:
Nothing's felt so real before	**Oooh—**
You got me scared to feel so sure	**Oooh-oooh—**
And I know every guy	**Oooh-oooh—**
Secretly wants you but ohh	**I want YOU!**
Oh-oh oh-oh-oh	
Oh oh-oh-oh	**Oh oh-oh-oh**

ALL: **Nobody loves you, loves you like me**
Nobody loves you, loves you like me
Nobody loves you, loves you like me
Girl, nobody loves you, not like I do
Nobody loves you, loves you like me
Nobody loves you, loves you like me
Nobody loves you, loves you like me
Girl, nobody loves you, not like I do

SONG: 'LET ME IN'

A Latin-style guitar hook.

HARRY: [Sydney], you're looking good tonight …
Name whatever you want, and it's yours
I'd give you anything
No regrets

TRUE CONNECTION: NO REGRETS!

HARRY: **I'll buy you shoes, makeup. Really. Cute. Pets**
I'd give you anything
If you just say yes

TRUE CONNECTION: I'LL GIVE YOU PETS!

HARRY: **Never ever ever ever giving up**
Till ya till ya till ya till ya let love win

Y'know y'know y'know what you need to do …
LET. ME. IN.
ALL: **Lalalala, let me in**
HARRY: **Open up and. LET. ME. IN.**
ALL: **Lalalala, let me in**
HARRY: **Just open yourself and—**
LET. ME. IN.
ALL: **Lalalala, let me in**
HARRY: **You got to, you need to—**
LET. ME. IN.
ALL: **Lalalala, let me in**
HARRY: **Let me into your … heart.**

SONG: 'COOL GIRL'

HARRY: How we all doing?

Crowd screams.

Hey, girl, you know exactly what you are.
You're a
Cool girl with the hair like that
With the jeans like that
With the
ALL: UGH like that
HARRY: **That's why we don't make it**
Past the door mat
When you kiss me like that
'Cause you're
ALL: Cool like that
HARRY: **Our little secret**
Hope you can keep it
My cool girl, cool girl
ALL: SHHHH!
My cool girl
HARRY: **We don't tell no-one**
That's why it's so fun
Cool girl, cool girl
ALL: SHHHH!
My cool girl

HARRY:	LEO:	REST OF TRUE CONNECTION:
Cool girl do it		
like I like		
Cool girl do it		
just like I like		
Cool girl do it	**Just like**	
like I like	**I li-i-i-ike**	
Cool girl do it	**Just like**	
just like I like	**I li-i-i-ike**	
Cool girl do it	*Hectic riff.*	**Ooh ooh my cool**
like I like		**girl**
Cool girl do it		**My cool gi-irl**
just like I like		**Ooh ooh my cool**
Cool girl do it		**girl**
do-ing it right		**My cool gi-irl**
Cool girl do it		
just like I like		

SONG: 'TOUCH THE MOON'

HARRY: [SYDNEY]!

Crowd screams.

I wanna get serious now.
We're living in some scary times.
Only we can make the change!
We are the generation
Who's gunna make all the change
REES: Gunna make all the change!
HARRY: **We need to spread the lovin'**
REES: Spread the lovin',
HARRY: **Save the world, before it's too late**

Big dance music drop.

ALL: [*spoken together*] DANCE!
HARRY: **And think of the children!**
ALL: [*spoken together*] DANCE!
HARRY: **Some children are not okay!**
ALL: [*spoken together*] DANCE!

HARRY: **Until we touch the moon!**
ALL: [*spoken together*] DANCE!
HARRY: **Until the world is saved!**

Inappropriately filthy drop.

ZAK *serenades an audience member in an aisle seat while grinding the air. The band dance filthily.*

ZAK: **Mmmm, dance, girl. Ch-ch-change the world**
Spread that love around. Let me see you twirl
Dance, girl. Ch-ch-change the world
You can do anything. But let me see you twirl
HARRY: **Girl, let me see you twirl**
And think of the children
MYLES: The children …
HARRY: **'Cause we are the generation**
MYLES: The generation …
HARRY: **Who's gunna touch the moon**
Think of the kids …

All of the band leave except HARRY. *A* ROADIE *brings him an acoustic guitar.*

'Ello 'ello!

Crowd screams.

Gosh, you look gorgeous.

Crowd screams.

The lads and I are really so grateful to you for having us at your place. In fact this might be, one of the best nights of our lives.

Crowd screams.

We've been getting a lot of requests on this tour about … a certain song. It seems you really like our song … 'Nobody'?
YAEL: [*demonic*] SING IT AGAINNNNNNNN!
HARRY: [Sydney]! Seeing as you look so beautiful tonight. I can't help myself, I need to tell you how I feel about you … one more time.

HARRY *plays an acoustic guitar.*

Let me see your phone lights up in the air!

HARRY: **I like your fingertips**
I like your soul

GEORGIA: [*yelling*] I want your dick! [*Or* 'I want your babies.']

HARRY: **Thinking of your messy hair**
I'm like WOAH

YAEL: [*yelling*] IIIIII WANT YOUR DICK! [*Or* 'IIIIII WANT YOUR BABIES!']

HARRY: **Forget the haters, why they so mean?**
'Cause you're the biggest babe they've ever seen
[*Calling to the crowd*] EVERYBODY!
Nobody loves you loves you like me
Nobody loves you loves you like me
Nobody loves you loves you like me
Girl, nobody loves you, not like I do
Goodnight [Sydney]!

The crowd goes wild. A sickening tinnitus sound. BRIANNA *and* JULES *stumble out of the concert, sobbing. This moment is exactly as it was last time.*

BRIANNA: I can't believe my phone died. Where's my flower crown?

JULES: DID YOU SEE HIM LOOK AT ME? HARRY DEFINITELY LOOKED AT ME. I'm. Actually. So. DEADDDDDDD.

SCENE 2—EDNA'S BEDROOM—3.42 A.M.

EDNA *opens her wardrobe to reveal* HARRY: *blindfolded, gagged, tied up. She's decked out the inside of the wardrobe with fairy lights, decorations and cushions.*

She tries to contain her excitement, fixes her hair and summons the courage to remove his blindfold. He takes in the sight of her. Surprised. She freezes.

HARRY *murmurs through the gag.* EDNA *holds up the chloroform rag as a threat. He shuts up. She gestures that she'll remove his gag if he's quiet. He nods.*

She gently removes it. A pause.

HARRY: Hi, love.

EDNA: Hhhh …

She cannot speak.

HARRY: What's your name?
EDNA: E … E …
HARRY: E?
EDNA: … Edna.
HARRY: Can you tell me where we are please?

She nods. She shakes her head. She's starstruck.

[*Calling out*] HELLO? HELLLP!
EDNA: Nononono! / Harry? No, please I don't want to—
HARRY: HELP MEEEEE! HELLLLLPPP!

EDNA *claps the rag to* HARRY*'s face and chloroforms him. He goes limp.*

SCENE 3—PANIC

A spooky choir coos. Frightened FANS *stare at their phones. Projected in the space, we see what they're all watching*:

NEWSREADER: This just in, a boy just eighteen years old …
Known to his fans simply as 'HARRY' …
Performed to ninety thousand last night …
Has since been. Reported …
FANS: Missing?

White noise.

Then: *the beat drops. Absolute chaos on stage. Videos of crying fans flood the screen.*

Ominous underscoring. EDNA *fakes a sick voice to* CAROLINE.

EDNA: I think I just need to stay in bed all day.
CAROLINE: [*offstage*] You should really try to go to school.
EDNA: Mum, EVERYthing hurts.
CAROLINE: It won't look good if you don't try to—
EDNA: Mum, I literally can't.

The beat resurges. NEWSREADERS *with various accents*:

NEWSREADER 1: One point four million fans have flooded London's Trafalgar Square …

NEWSREADER 2: '… have flocked to Times Square …'
NEWSREADER 3: '… are holding vigil in Tiananmen Square …'

Ominous underscoring. EDNA *at her computer.*

SALTY: Hey. Friend. You there? I feel sick to my stomach. Have you seen this video of his mom crying?

EDNA *watches the video, struggling.*

This is so spooky, right? I can't believe that we were JUST researching a fic where a fan kidnaps HARRY and now he's … gone?! Did we like, curse him?

The sound of the video:

HARRY'S MUM: [*voice-over*] Whoever has him, please, give me back my son.

JULES *and* BRIANNA *at school.*

JULES: He's dead, I can feel it.
BRIANNA: Don't, Jules!
JULES: I could literally just die anytime. I'm fourteen and I have never known LOVE!
BRIANNA: Jules … you're so pretty. You're gunna get in love so easily
JULES: / No I won't.
BRIANNA: I can't believe I didn't get ANY pics! As if my phone died. Can you send me the ones you took?
JULES: Oh, Bri, I forgot to tell you—I'm so sorry, but I had to delete them to save space.
BRIANNA: [*quiet and devastated*] But we … I planned that outfit for ages.
JULES: Just post a picture of you in the same clothes and say it was the night of the concert.
BRIANNA: [*swallowing her devastation*] Look, there's a vigil after school tomorrow.
JULES: What's a vigil?
BRIANNA: Eddy would know? 'Meet at [local landmark] at four p.m. This will be a safe space to support each other through this scary time and share GLUTEN-FREE PIZZA!' Do you wanna go?

They go. CAROLINE *calls* EDNA *from work (hospital).* EDNA *fakes a sick voice.*

CAROLINE: Hi, darling, how are you feeling?

EDNA: Yeah, still not good.

CAROLINE: Maybe I should come home then?

EDNA: No! No! I mean I'm not good but I'm not worse. Honestly There's no reason for you to leave work—

A cacophony of anxious fans' voices rises up and into:

SONG: 'PANIC'

LILY: **Terrorists, Dad said it's terrorists. That's what he said!**

DOM: **My psychic auntie says he's DEFS not dead**

SALTY: **But if it were terrorists, someone would claim it**
Publish a video, which would explain what
They wanted, their demands

GRETA: What if they've cut off his PENIS?!

ASH: **Maybe it's a just publicity stunt?**

SALTY: **But they've lost so much money on ticket refunds**

GRETA & LILY: **And his mum looks REALLY sad!**

SALTY: **I don't think it can be fake**

ASH: **What if he just like, ran?**

LILY: **He'd never!**

GRETA: **He'd never do that to the fans!**

SALTY: What if he did something else?

LILY: Like what else?

SALTY: **What if he did something to himself?**

ALL BUT SALTY: Don't say that!

SALTY: I think we need to prepare for the worst. I made this spreadsheet. You put in your name and time zone and then you can see who else might be awake if you need a chat. We need to take care of each other and—

LILY: What we NEED to do is find whoever took him and MAKE THEM PAYYYYYY!

SCENE 4—EDNA'S BEDROOM

EDNA *wears latex gloves. She holds a sandwich and a chloroform-soaked rag.*

EDNA: I'm going to feed this to you. But not because I want to be creepy, just because I have to. If I wanted to be creepy I wouldn't use gloves, so …

She dies of embarrassment, then gestures to her rag. HARRY *nods. She removes his gag.*

HARRY: Sorry, love, do you mind taking a bite first?

EDNA: [*horrified*] Ohmygod, of course. [*Taking a bite*] It's not. Poison. It's actually your favourite, so—

HARRY *begins devouring the sandwich. It's a bit sexual.* EDNA *quakes.*

HARRY: Darling, can you tell me why I'm here?

She nods reluctantly. She takes a position like she's about to audition, and gets out a set of index cards.

By the way … you have really beautiful eyes.

She drops all her cards. She gathers them, embarrassed, and begins her pitch.

SONG: 'BECOME BRAND NEW'

EDNA: **They just love you 'cause you're famous but I don't care**
I see past the branding, I see past the [*gulp*] hair
I see a different person hiding in plain sight
And at first I might sound crazy, but you'll see that I'm right

HARRY: About what love?

EDNA: **I know about your meds. I know you feel lost**

HARRY: Howja know that, love?

EDNA: **They're using you like a puppet and don't think of the cost**

HARRY: Who's 'they'?

EDNA: **But how can you break free when everyone knows you?**

HARRY: … Right?

EDNA: **The only option, is to: Run. Become. Brand. New.**

HARRY: What do you mean 'run'?

EDNA: **Think it through.**
No matter how much you want to quit

The fans will never quit you
But you don't have to live as others decide
In hiding we'll finally have nothing to hide

You're not trapped anymore, Harry.

HARRY: So … I can go?

EDNA: No! I mean, now you're free.

HARRY: Free to … go?

EDNA: No, I mean, you *were* trapped. In the band. Right? But now you're—

HARRY: But … I *am* trapped. I'm like … tied up?

EDNA: I mean, technically … yes—but you *will* be free when we go … on the run.

HARRY: Um. But … how would we go … 'on the run'?
We'd need … money, we'd need transport, we'd need—

EDNA *pulls the following out of a backpack of supplies.*

EDNA: We'd need …

Hair dye, keys to the car
Protein bars, spare sim cards

Oh, this is a fake baby so everyone believes we're … actually a couple. Anyway!

Vitamins, knives, bribes for the police
Tea bags, Ziplocs
Makeup, mace spray, multiple wigs
… Some shower flip flops
I got fake noses, plastic ponchos
In case it rains, Panadol for aches and pains
A whole first-aid kit, fake tattoos
Raisins, almonds, tiny shampoos

HARRY: How did you figure this all out?

EDNA: … Internet?

HARRY: But where did you—? How did you get all this stuff?

EDNA: How did I afford it?

I've never been rich
Like you, I'm a scholarship kid
But I knew I had to save you
So I just did what I had to

'Cause the chances you don't take
Are the monsters that you make
So I scraped, and I saved
And I stole some stuff too
Including the van
That I taught myself to drive
Which wasn't easy. To do. Off YouTube.

HARRY: I think that officially makes you my biggest fan.

EDNA: I'm not a—Harry, I didn't do this because I'm a 'crazy fan'. I did this to save you.

HARRY: Right. But from what, love?

EDNA: The fans?

HARRY: But I love / the …

EDNA: Your life? Being told what to do all the time?
Look, I know you're not used to admitting it to anyone, Harry, but I know how you feel … and I know what it's like.

HARRY: What's it like?

EDNA: **I know you think we live opposite lives**
On opposite sides of this rock
But I—

HARRY: Rock?

EDNA: … As in … the earth? The rock is the … earth. It's a metaph—

HARRY: Oh! Yeah! Right! Sorry, go ahead.

EDNA: I was just saying, I know you think we're different but—
I know what it feels like to be under pressure
To wish that it all would just stop
To have no REAL friends
No-one you can trust
Your mum's hopes are on your shoulders
But you'll never be enough
To feel like you're half alive
Like you're swallowing a scream
While everyone tells you
Who you should try to be
Don't you wish that you could just break free?

HARRY *nods.*

… Then why not? Let's just … go.

The longest pause in the world.

HARRY: … Okay.
You're right.
Let's go.
Fake smiles, tight chest, 'living the dream'
But really dreamt of just running, from the sea of screams
I guess I never realised, that I don't have to live this lie
But now I see life could be so much more
Been trapped so long, and now I see a door

EDNA: **Um, that was really sudden.**
Are you sure?

HARRY: **I can't believe I didn't see before**

EDNA: **… Are you really sure?**

HARRY: **How could I have been so wrong? I give you all my trust**
'Cause now the only real

A long sexy riff.

Thi-i-i-ing
Is us

EDNA: WHAT?!

HARRY: **Is uuuuuus**

A CHOIR *sings. Epic strings.*

EDNA: **Oh my god … Oh my god … OH MY GOD?!**

HARRY: **Just uuuuuus, baby, just us**

EDNA *starts untying him. They sing to each other. In love.*

HARRY & EDNA: **Is uuuus. Uuuus. Just uuuus. Uuuuuu—**

He's standing now. Singing into her face. He leans in to kiss her when—

He shoves her to the ground and runs.

EDNA: [*calling after him*] HARRY!

She grabs her chloroform rag and tears after him.

SCENE 5—LIFE OR DEATH

Scared FANS *fill the space, lit by their phones.*

SONG: 'LIFE OR DEATH'

FANS: **Thi-hi-his is life or death**
I can't even! What is breath?
Mum, I'm really scared …
What if he's actually … (dead)

The FANS *sing a chilling underscore. A bro-ey radio host:*

RADIO BRO: I mean, my daughter has lost her mind—
No, I'm not, I'm not being sexist—I'm just saying that—
Well, you wouldn't, you wouldn't see boys going on like this—
Or, y'know—listening to that music in the first place.

SALTY *messages* EDNA.

SALTY: Hey! You're the only one we can't get hold of, so …

I just wanted to make sure you had a link to this petition. It's to stop the hashtag CutForHarry. It's been trending for the last four hours and we wanna try to get it disabled …

Just, let me know you're okay, yeah?

CAROLINE *is on a break from her night shift as a nurse. She's watching a video, worried.*

NEWSREADER: In the wake of the crisis, [Kids Help Line] has set up a dedicated hotline for grieving fans. Today, the head of the organisation, Sue Crellen, gave a public statement on the matter:

SUE CRELLEN: [*voice-over*] It's important for adults to get their head around the fact that—the distress that these young people are experiencing is very real. For some young people, who have a tough time at school, or at home—they might listen to Harry's music—and feel like they have a friend. And so for him to just, disappear—it's a very serious loss. For some, it will be their first encounter with grief. And so I ask parents, please, don't undermine this pain. Even if you don't understand it.

CAROLINE *goes.* JULES *appears, alone in her room. She takes a phone call.*

JULES: Hi, Dad! No, it's fine, I wasn't doing anything.
… Yeah?
Oh.
That's okay. I'll just see you next weekend.
Oh, right, yeah that's what I meant—the one after.
No seriously, it's fine. So how've you been?
Oh yep, no worries. Take the call. Alright, love y—

BRIANNA, *alone in her room. She's wearing her exact outfit from the concert and trying to take selfies. She checks them: they're all shit. She messages* JULES.

BRIANNA: Heyyyy, was my makeup last night, like was it more *pretty* or was it more *hot*?

JULES *is also trying to take selfies*

JULES: Um … it was more … pretty. Like it *was* hot but it was more pretty than hot.

BRIANNA: [*devastated*] Oh. Should it have been more—?

JULES: Hey, random question: do you reckon guys notice if your bra strap is showing in pics? Or do they only notice if they can actually see a bit of bra—like poking out the top? Ohmygod, have you seen this?

BRIANNA: [*reading a post*] 'Posting this pic of us on the last happy night of our lives—the concert where my husband was last seen. Stay strong and remember, #FansAreFamily'.
It's amazing how all these strangers are like, binding together.

JULES: It's amazing that she thinks she fits those shorts.

BRIANNA *looks down at her thighs with devastation.*

SCENE 6—EDNA'S BEDROOM

EDNA: I understand why you'd be angry with me right now, and that is completely fair.

EDNA *enters with* HARRY, *who's in a wheelie chair. She's bound him to it with what she could find: extension cords, Christmas lights, duct tape.*

I think if you just listen to my plan, and really think about it—you'll see that I am not actually weird—that this is not a crazy idea. It makes more sense than the life you're living right now, and it is the ONLY chance you'll ever get to truly start again.

HARRY *is having a coughing fit.*

So—Oh, sorry, here's some water.

EDNA *removes his gag to give a sip of water. It was a trick.*

HARRY: You and me? Are two very different rocks.

EDNA: What?

HARRY: We are not the same rock, and we never will be.

EDNA: Why are you talking about rocks?

HARRY: Because you keep talking about them!

EDNA: Wha—oh! no, I meant that we're *on* the same rock, as in—

HARRY: We are different rocks and we are different people! Okay? And all of this? Doesn't make me want you. Look, I get it. You think that if I fall in love with you then you'll be cool and famous—

EDNA: No—I'm not doing this to be famous?

HARRY: And you finally won't feel like a loser.

EDNA: What?

HARRY: But, darlin', this? Is not hot!—

EDNA: I'm not trying to be / hot … I'm …

HARRY: It's gross! I would NEVER date ANYONE who did this. Okay? So you can call the police right now.

EDNA: Harry, I know / I accidentally scared you and I'm sorry for that—

HARRY: The longer you wait to call them the worse this is going to be for you.

EDNA: But if you just listen to the plan—

HARRY: No, YOU Listen to ME. This is a very serious crime with VERY. Serious. Consequences.

HARRY: You realise that everyone in the world will watch what you did. / How you dressed up, followed me into a TOILET, how you gassed me and TOOK me. They'll release the footage. /You realise that, right? There are cameras everywhere backstage. When they come here, not if but … WHEN they come here—	EDNA: But I— No but— I took out the cameras. I—There weren't any in the bathroom anyway that's why I—

HARRY: I am NEVER running away with you.
BE. REALISTIC.
The longer you keep me here, the worse it'll be for you. So, Emma. Up to you.
Just how much do you wanna ruin your life?

'Emma' shatters her. She tries to hold it together.

EDNA: … Do you … want some more water?
HARRY: You're disgusting.

EDNA *hides so she can cry.*

SCENE 7—DISGUSTING

Alone, JULES *looks at herself.*

SONG: 'DISGUSTING'

VERSE 1

JULES: **When I smile**
In photos, I notice
My eyes do this thing at the sides
They look all scrunched up
Like two little bumholes
I wish they weren't mine

Mum says looks aren't everything
But as if they're even not though
Your looks are the way people look at you
How they decide if you're someone
They'd like to actually know

Mum says I'm still growing,
But I'm already overgrown
No-one told me about this bit
Will I ever get to stop, oh, just pretending to feel hot?
'Cause what. If this. Is it.
What if I'm …

CHORUS 1

Eye broccoli
What if people call me
Frumpty dumpty
With a butt that's lumpy?

Mungbean
A yak or a fat bitch?
A feral mole or an
Acne sandwich?

Fugly
With undescended testes
Cankles and a
Triple chin

What if I'm just
Disgusting?

VERSE 2

Alone, BRIANNA *looks at herself.*

BRIANNA: **Pip has boobs,**
But Jules says one's too big
And she'll never get a boyfriend now …

But I'm still jealous
'Cause I'm flat as a pancake
And Pip looks great in photos
But I don't know how

Mum says I'm still growing
But what if I never grow?
I'm too old to have no tits
And I'm tired of not knowing
If this skin suit will ever feel like home
'Cause what. If this. Is it.
What if I'm …

CHORUS 2

They sing simultaneously.

BRIANNA: **Ugly**
Face like a donkey
With my
Legs all stumpy

… A minger
Or a fat bitch?
With a
Nose like a witch

What if I'm festy?
What if my breath stinks?
Thighs like cottage cheese
Bingo wings

What if I'm just
Disgusting?

JULES: **Eye broccoli**
What if people call me
Frumpty dumpty
With a butt that's lumpy?

Mungbean
A yak or a fat bitch?
A feral mole or an
Acne sandwich?

Fugly
With undescended testes
Cankles and a
Triple chin

What if I'm just
Disgusting?

CHORUS 3

FANS *sing the overlapping choruses. The girls descant:*

EDNA: **What if he's right? What, what if I'm—**
What if I'm just … disgusting?

BRIANNA: **In this skin I'm someone I don't wanna be.**

JULES: **Will I ever get to stop, just pretending to feel hot**

BRIANNA: **I'm too old to have no tits.**

JULES: **What if this is it?**

EDNA: **How could I, be so dumb**
What if I can't take back all that I've done
What if I'm just …

ALL: **What if I'm just …**
Disgusti—

EDNA *opens her laptop.*

SCENE 8—DIRECT MESSAGES

SALTY: TELL ME YOU ARE ALIVE OR I WILL HAVE TO USE MY DARK INTERNET POWERS TO FIND YOUR LOCATION AND SEND SOMEONE TO CHECK ON YOU!

EDNA: I'm alive!

SALTY: Where have you / been?

EDNA: Salty, I need a new ending.

SALTY: Wh … To what?

EDNA: To the fic we wrote where the girl kidnaps Harry. I've realised that there's no way it would end with them falling in love. Right? 'Cause he'd hate her. I'd hate her.

SALTY: Um, babe, I REALLY don't think we should post that story right now.

EDNA: I'm not going to post it, I just need to re-write it. To, um … cope with everything. Please can you just help me?

SALTY: Well … okay.

EDNA: I want to write a new ending where they don't run away together, but where—she let's him go. But also, where um, no-one ever finds out what she's done?

SALTY: Ew. Boring.

EDNA: I just need help figuring out like, how she would do that.

SALTY: BETTER IDEA! What if the fans DO find out that she's kidnapped him, and then thousands of them storm her house and rip her arms off?! Oh my god, people would LOVE THAT RIGHT NOW!

EDNA: No, Salty, I really want it to end with her still alive.

What I need to know is—how could she, realise what she's done, and then, like, un-kidnap him.

SALTY: NEW IDEA! What if, she realises what she's done, SO THEN—she calls the cops on herself and like—goes to jail!

Because then, she'd end up how he started: trapped! And also, famous? Think about it, the whole world would see her as a psycho for the rest of her life. She'd spend forever being totally misunderstood and depressed. I would LOVE that SYMMETRY!

EDNA: I don't want her to go to jail, Salty, I want no-one to ever find out what she did.

SALTY: Well, then … her only option is to kill him …

EDNA: …

SALTY: 'Cause if he lives, he's just going to tell. So she'd have to get rid of him. And like, hide his body.

EDNA: … How would she do that?

SALTY: Well, suffocate him, and then dissolve his body in acid? It's not my favourite ending, but it IS a powerful metaphor for how his management are working him to literal death.

EDNA *stares at a pillow in her room. She picks it up. Contemplates it as a weapon.*

EDNA: Okay … thanks, Salty. I gotta go.

Beat.

SALTY: We all miss you on the group.

Beat.

Hey, um, here's is my number. If you want it. You can [Whatsapp] me any time. It'll come up with my parentally assigned name. Jonathan, that's me.

Look, if you're in [city], then maybe you should join one of the search parties for Harry? It'll remind you how powerful we are? I know it's hard right now, but I promise you, we WILL find whoever did this.

CAROLINE: [*offstage*] Eddy? You up?

SCENE 9—EDNA'S BEDROOM

CAROLINE *is at the door.* EDNA *chloroforms* HARRY *and coughs over the sound of his whimpers. She shoves his chair in the wardrobe. Simultaneously*:

EDNA: DON'T COME IN, I'M NAKED!

CAROLINE: [*offstage*] Eddy, are you alright?

EDNA: MUM, WAIT! YOU WOKE ME UP! JUST LET ME GET DRESSED-A.

CAROLINE: [*offstage*] What's that sound?

EDNA *meets her mum at the door just in time.*

EDNA: [*in a fake sick voice*] What? MUM, I'm sleeping.

CAROLINE: Sweetheart, can we … talk?

EDNA: Now?! It's like midnight.

CAROLINE: Darling, I know about Harry.

EDNA: What?

EDNA *is frozen.*

CAROLINE: It's just awful. But, hey, that security footage looks really promising.

EDNA: What footage?

CAROLINE: You know—from after the show? There's a really little guy in a black hoodie who loads a big suitcase into a van without number plates. He must have passed as one of the stage crew. I reckon they'll find that van in no time and Harry'll be right as rain.

EDNA: Mum, can I please just sleep?

CAROLINE: Okay. One hug goodnight and I'll go.

CAROLINE *hugs* EDNA. EDNA *resists, but then hugs her mum back like it's the last time she ever will.* CAROLINE *holds her and sings.*

SONG: 'BRAVE THING'

VERSE 1

CAROLINE: **I can't imagine. What. It's like**
To lose someone you love so much

EDNA: Mum—

CAROLINE: **'Cause if I tried. To imagine it**
I'd have to think of losing you, my love

Oh, it's a brave thing to love
To have something to lose
That could just tear you apart
And I've known that since the day that I had you

EDNA *tries to break the hug but* CAROLINE *pulls her in.*

CHORUS 1

CAROLINE: **I know you're growing up, and you need space**
But I hope you'll never hide, when you aren't okay

'Cause I love you in a way that
Nothing in this world could stop

And I'll be here
No matter what

EDNA: Mum, I'm really tired so—

CAROLINE: **No matter what**

VERSE 2

CAROLINE: **I know I tell you off sometimes**
And tell you what to do
But it isn't because
I'm disappointed by you

I'm so proud of who you are
Can't believe that I'm your mum
And every day I am in awe of the person you've beccoooome

EDNA: Mum, seriously, right now isn't the time for a / chat—

CHORUS 2

CAROLINE: **I know you're growing up**
And you need space
But I hope you never hide
When you aren't okay

'Cause I love you in a way that
Nothing in this world could stop
And I'll be here
No matter wha—

Desperate, EDNA *explodes*:

EDNA: MUM! CAN YOU JUST LET ME SLEEP!

Wounded, CAROLINE *goes to leave. Then decides to say*:

VERSE 3

CAROLINE: **It's a brave thing to love**
To have something to lose
But the thing that tears me apart
Is when you don't see that all I'm trying to do

Is give you everything
I'd take a bullet for you, I wouldn't have to think

'Cause in my eyes you're
The most precious thing

Oh, Eddy. No matter what
Nobody loves you like—

EDNA: MUM! I'M SICK AND I JUST WANT TO SLEEP! HOW MANY TIMES DO I HAVE TO ASK?!

CAROLINE: Alright.

But tomorrow—I'd like you to try to go to school, and then if he's still gone in the afternoon, how about we go to the vigil together? [*Getting nothing*] You can ask Jules and Bri too?

EDNA: [*unable to look at her*] I don't think I'll be well enough, Mum.

CAROLINE: Alright.

Sweet dreams, Teddy.

EDNA *watches* CAROLINE *leave. In the sound design, a scary cacophony of angry fans' whispers rises up.* EDNA *opens her laptop again and becomes lit only by the screen. She stares at it anxiously. The whispers rise up, and become more clear*: *'Whoever did this has to pay', 'The sicko who did this should rot in hell'—finally, soaring above the noise, we hear* SALTY*'s voice reverberate*:

SALTY: Her only option … is to kill him.

SCENE 10—JUSTICE

A video of NAZ, *aged twelve, is projected across the space. She's staring into the camera, vlogging.* EDNA *watches her.*

At some point during this intro, NAZ *walks on stage, holding up her phone, as if she's making the video right now. She wears a school uniform.*

SONG: 'JUSTICE'

INTRO

NAZ: **I do not believe we are**
Born evil
Whoever did this is in pain
And I'm sorry someone tore a hole in your heart
If I could meet you

I would ho-old you, so you could feel love
I could kiss each of your eyelids

Before slowly removing each of them
With toenail clippers
Now can you see what you're doing to us?
Now that you know what love feels like do you
Understand what you've destroyed?
Because you stole my husband and now you're going to pay the price for it, you piece of TRASSSSSH!

CAM, TAL *and* ROSA *appear in unexpected parts of the space. It's scary. They all look thirteen to fifteen and wear different school uniforms. They wield homemade signs: 'VAN SEARCH PARTY MEET HERE', 'FIND OUR PORKCHOP'. We are at the vigil* BRIANNA *has been hearing about.*

CHORUS 1

ALL: **Tease us, and hate us**
But don't underestimate us
'Cause we're in love
TAL: And I found Mum's peroxide
ROSA: **We're coming to get what's ours**
It's as simple as that
We want
ALL: JUSTICE! HARRY!
NAZ: **And your kneecaps**

Crunch.

BRIANNA *appears, searching.*

CAM: Would you like some gluten-free pizza?
BRIANNA: [*shy*] … I'm Brianna. I'm looking for my friend Jules—
NAZ: Until we find them you just stick with us, yeah?
ROSA: How are you feeling about it all?
CAM: You can answer honestly, hun, this is a safe space.

VERSE 1

BRIANNA: **It's been the darkest week of my entire life**
Every second he's gone I feel a part of me die

ROSA: **We need to find whoever has him**
Need to go to their place

NAZ: **We need to demand that they hand us our husband**
Or we'll rearrange their faaaaaaaace

ALL: HEY!

CHORUS 2

ALL: **Tease us and hate us**
But don't underestimate us
'Cause we're in love

NAZ: And I found a chainsaw.

ALL: **We're coming to get what's ours**
It's as simple as that
We want
JUSTICE! HARRY!

ROSA: **And your kneecaps**

Crunch.

BRIANNA: Last night I was sad about it and my brother just kept laughing.

CAM: Ohmygod, mine literally did too. Didn't I say?!

ROSA: He literally exactly did!

BRIANNA: Right? And it's like, not funny.

TAL: Our hearts are literally broken, you guys. The only thing I can do to stay sane right now is imagine what I'd do to the dickhat that did this. Before taking him to the police, I'd take him to my basement. And I know exactly. What. I'd. Say.

VERSE 2

Prepubescent punisher
Coming to have some fun witcha
Wanna see even your fingernails sweating
Restore your phone to factory settings
Here's Harry's lyrics, you have an hour to learn them
For every wrong word I'll put a nail in your sternum

Six nail gun hits.

CAM: Hold up, hold up, hold up.

The track cuts.

Ladies, I appreciate the enthusiasm. But can we talk about the real shit-uation here? The entire world is literally laughing at our grief. You wanna know why the media isn't covering the search for Harry anymore? It's because they're too busy DRAGGING us for BEING in LOVE.

VERSE 3

CAM: **THEY. THINK. WE'RE. JUST.**
Pimply preteens with a propensity for panic
Predictably predisposed to particularly manic
ATTACKS of hysteria, batshit behaviour
These little girls think
This boy is their saviour

ROSA: **Allow me to stress**
We're not insane or depressed
We're just in pain and expressing it
What's to gain from suppressing it?

TAL: **Why should we hide our feelings**
Because they annoy you?
OH! Because it isn't what the boys do?!

BRIANNA: **Wait, let me get this straight**
If my brother loves a footballer
That's normal, natural
Yelling at the telly
NO! That's not weird at all
It's fine if Dad cries
'Cause some guy didn't catch a ball
But if I cry over Harry I'm a freak?

ALL: WHAT?!

NAZ: **A group of passionate women**
They must be crazy bitches
Wait, isn't that the excuse that they used to
Burn the witches?

BRIANNA: **They try to teach us**
That us female creatures
Should be fluffy little peaches
Apologetic and speechless

And every billboard preaches
The lesson that we are less. Than.
So we waste time fussing over features
Wondering what will impress. Men!

CAM: **No day on this earth is promised to you**
So with the brief time you have here, what you gunna do?
Ridicule me for what makes me feel good?
Tell me what it is that I shouldn't or should

ROSA: **Be doing with my time?**

NAZ: **Be holding in my heart?**

BRIANNA: **Be singing in my room when school is really HARD?**
Oh, tell me more about my shitty taste
My life's all mine, so yours is yours to waste

ALL: **OHHHHHHHH SNAP!**

BREAKDOWN

The vigil becomes a protest. Amazing dance break. Pizza boxes everywhere. BRIANNA *grabs a megaphone. She's been awakened.*

Meanwhile, in her bedroom, EDNA *clutches her pillow and a teddy bear. As she sings, she tries to bring herself to practise suffocating the bear, in preparation for what she must do next …*

ENSEMBLE 1:	ENSEMBLE 2:	EDNA:
Tease us [*x 4*]	**JUSTICE**	
Hate us [*x4*]	**JUSTICE**	
Don't	**JUSTICE [*x 2*]**	
underestimate us	**JUSTICE [*x 4*]**	
	JUSTICE [*x 2*]	**What I've done is**
We're in love	**JUSTICE [*x 2*]**	**done**
	JUSTICE [*x 2*]	**And there's**
And we want	**JUSTICE [*x 2*]**	**nowhere to run**
	JUSTICE [*x 2*]	**Like it or not**
And we want	**JUSTICE [*x 2*]**	**What choice have**
	KNEECAPS [*x 2*]	**I got?**
And we also want	**KNEECAPS [*x 2*]**	**Ohhh**

EDNA: **It's kill him or get caught**

CHORUS 3

ALL: **Te-e-e-ease us and hate us**
But don't underestimate us
'Cause we're in love
NAZ: And I'm THIRSTY FOR BLOOD!
ALL: **We're coming to get what's ours**
It's as simple as that
We want
[*Shouted*] JUSTICE!
BRIANNA: [*shouted*] RESPECT!
NAZ: **A NOOSE ON YOUR NECK**
ALL: [*shouted*] HARRY
ROSA: [*shouted*] Our CUPCAKE!
TAL: **SERIOUSLY GIVE HIM BEK—**
ALL: **We want to make a difference.**
To something greater than ourselves
We want what's oursssss
NAZ: **And your kneecaps as well**

Crunch.

SCENE 11—JULES' BEDROOM

BRIANNA *bursts in.*

JULES: Why are you here?
BRIANNA: Have you seen my texts? … Jules?

JULES *is distracted by something on her phone.*

JULES: What?
BRIANNA: Why did you run off and jump on that random bus without me? … Jules?

BRIANNA *demands her attention.*

JULES: … What?
BRIANNA: I thought you were doing a weird joke and I'd see you at the vigil, so I went on my own and I looked for you everywhere and you weren't anywhere. Why did you … ditch me? JULES!
JULES: Bri, I'm in the middle of something.

BRIANNA *grabs* JULES' *phone and reads it.* JULES *tries to get it back.*

BRIANNA: WHO THE HELL IS KYLE?

JULES: My boyfriend, okay.

BRIANNA: I saw you three hours ago and you didn't have a boyfriend.

JULES: Well, I met him on the bus.

BRIANNA: ONE DOWN, FOUR TO GO?! As in True Connection?!

JULES: Bri, what I say to my boyfriend is private.

BRIANNA: How can you SAY that about Harry? About anyone?

JULES: Oh relax, Bri. Harry wasn't that great. Kyle hopes he's dead.

JULES *has her phone again.*

BRIANNA: The vigil was great.

JULES: [*sniggering*] Kyle called it the virgin festival.

BRIANNA: It wasn't a virgin festival! It was … It was … Everyone was so nice to me. I didn't know anyone and they were so nice. And I thought—oh, is this what it's like to have friends who aren't slack to you ALL THE TIME?

JULES: What are you saying?

BRIANNA: I'm saying that you should apologise to me.

JULES: Okay. Sorry.

BRIANNA: And Edna.

JULES: What?

BRIANNA: You should call her.

JULES: She's fine, Bri, she's just sick.

BRIANNA: Do you know that?

JULES: Either that or she's pretending to be so she can stay home and write her psycho stories.

BRIANNA: Jules. She hasn't replied to a single call or text from me in two days. How do we know that she hasn't 'HASHTAG cut for Harry'?

JULES: She … she wouldn't.

BRIANNA: Wouldn't she? Ever since she stopped sitting with us she's looked *actually* depressed, Jules. And every time she was near us you'd start talking about the concert just so she could hear—

JULES: You went to the concert too—

BRIANNA: And I wish I didn't. I wish I'd said sorry and I wish we were all still friends.

JULES: Well, what do you want me to do?!

BRIANNA: I want you to call her and apologise.

JULES *is nervous.*

BRIANNA: Call her.

Reluctantly, JULES *does.*

SCENE 12—EDNA'S BEDROOM

EDNA *holds her phone. Sees who's calling. Lets it ring out. She turns to* HARRY.

EDNA: [*crumpling*] I'm … I'm really, really sorry.
You're right, Harry. Um. What I did was wrong. So I'm going to call the police and, um … give them my address.

SONG: 'SILLY LITTLE GIRL'

VERSE 1

EDNA: **I'll call. They'll come**
And in an hour my whole life will be … done
Forever I'll become
'That silly little girl'

You'll tell them … what I did
You'll tell them who I am
But you'll never have known me
And the whole world will only
Ever see me as just
'That silly little girl'
But …

CHORUS 1

You. Said.
You loved me
In my headphones
In the lonely black

You. Said.
You loved me
And I—

VERSE 2

I wanted everything to change
There wasn't one thing that I'd keep
I can't have any of it now
My life is just a memory

But the saddest part is not
That you can't love me
It's that I let you contain
All I thought that I could be

But that was every single story
I'd ever been told
Unless I was half of someone else
I could never be whole

And you don't get it
'Cause in your world
No-one's ever sold you lies
Made just for silly little girls

CHORUS 2

You. Said.
You loved me
Held my hand
In the lonely black

You. Said.
You loved me
And I—
I loved you back.

POST-CHORUS

The ensemble sing like a sad choir. EDNA *descants.*

VERSE 3

Tell Brianna that she's beautiful
In ways she isn't counting
Tell Jules she's so powerful,
In ways she isn't trying to be

Tell my mum she's better
Than I ever let her believe
That I wish I thanked her
For all she's given me

Don't waste the freedom that you have
Don't think you don't have a choice
The words that you sing matter
Choose how you use your voice

Don't tell us that we're pretty
Like it's the only thing to be
You don't know what it's like
You don't know how to see

You'll never know what it's like to be
Told. You're just a 'silly little girl'

EDNA *presses three numbers on her phone and dials.*

OPERATOR: [*voice-over*] 'You have dialled Emergency Triple Zero. Would you like police, fire and rescue or ambulance?

EDNA: I … I …

OPERATOR: [*voice-over*] Hello, can you hear me?

EDNA: Police, please.

A knock at the door.

BRIANNA: [*offstage*] EDNA?

EDNA *freezes.*

EDNA: Go away!

EDNA *hangs up. She scrambles to gag* HARRY *and close the wardrobe.*

BRIANNA: [*offstage*] Edna, we came to tell you something.

JULES: [*offstage*] Yeah.

EDNA: [*to* HARRY] Shhh. Please. I'll call the cops after, but just don't.

BRIANNA: … Edna?

EDNA: GO AWAY!

BRIANNA: WE CAME TO TELL YOU WE'RE SORRY. EDNA?

EDNA *blasts a True Connection song.* JULES *and* BRIANNA *burst in.*

[*Over the music*] EDNA—
EDNA: WHY ARE YOU HERE? GO AWAY?!
BRIANNA: WE CAME TO TELL YOU THAT—
EDNA: I'M REALLY SICK AND. CONTAGIOUS!
BRIANNA: THAT WE'RE—
EDNA: SO YOU NEED TO GO!

BRIANNA *shuts the laptop. The song stops.*

BRIANNA: We wanted to tell you we're sorry, Edna. Jules?
JULES: Yeah.
EDNA: GO AWAY!
JULES: Um! We're just trying to—

A banging sound. The wardrobe doors go crazy on their hinges.

What the hell?

HARRY *moans.* EDNA *attempts to cover the sound by pretending to retch.*

What the hell? … Brianna?

BRIANNA *puts it together.*

BRIANNA: Oh my god.

EDNA *retches.*

EDNA: LEAVE!

She retches again.

I'm gunna be sick!
JULES: Oh my god.
BRIANNA: Oh my god.
JULES: Oh my god.
BRIANNA: Oh my god.

JULES *pushes past* EDNA *and opens the wardrobe.*

Time stands still.

JULES: This …
Is …
The BEST.

BRIANNA *and* EDNA *look at her like WTF?*

BRIANNA: Edna … you?

JULES: This is the coolest thing that's happened to my whole life.
I had you wrong, babe.

BRIANNA: Edna, what have you—?

EDNA: Shhhhh! Please, Bri, please—

JULES: Let's keep him!

BRIANNA: JULES?! We have to tell someone …

JULES: Not yet, Bri! He's right here!
Ohmygod, he's right here.

JULES *steps towards him.*

BRIANNA: Jules, don't.

EDNA: Jules, don't.

BRIANNA & EDNA: Jules? Jules … JULES!

JULES *removes his blindfold.*

JULES: Hi, Harry, I'm Jules. Juliet, but people call me Jules—you might recognise me from the concert?

EDNA: Jules. Step away.

JULES: Edna, he doesn't look very comfortable.

BRIANNA: [*to* EDNA] Why didn't you call us?

JULES: Let me undo some of those buttons so you can breathe.

She sits on his lap.

He's so cute! [*Getting out her phone*] I wanna take a picture.

BRIANNA & EDNA: DON'T, JULES!

They swat it out of her hand.

JULES: Seriously, guys, chill.

EDNA: Bri, get her away from him.

JULES: Bri, chill.

BRIANNA *is torn.* HARRY *hyperventilates.*

[*To* HARRY] It's okay … I'll remove your gag if you don't scream—Alright, babe?

JULES *removes his gag and he sinks his teeth into her hand. She screams.*

HARRY *won't let go. Blood is gushing.* EDNA *goes to chloroform him with her rag, but before she gets there,* BRIANNA *grabs Edna's laptop and whacks* HARRY *on the head, knocking him out cold.*

They all freeze. Tense underscoring.

SONG: 'THE WOODS'

BRIANNA: **Ohmygod. Ohmygod. Ohmygod.** [*Repeating*]
EDNA: **No. No. No. No. No. No. No. No.** [*Repeating*]
JULES: **Holy … Mother of … JESUSSSSSS**
ALL: **OH MY AC-TU-AL GOD!**
BRIANNA & EDNA: **Think! / What do we do?** [*Repeating*]
JULES: **I can't go to prison, I'm way to young!**
Maybe we have to … Maybe we have to um—
Kill him?
BRIANNA & EDNA: What? NO!
Nonononononono [*Repeating*]
JULES: **Well, it's him or us**
BRIANNA: **What have we done?!**
JULES: **I don't know! I don't know!** [*Repeating*]
EDNA: **WHY DID YOU EVEN COME?**
Why did you just barge in?
I told you to stay outside
JULES: **We just wanted, I wanted**
To tell you that I'm …

Pause.

I'm …
So so SO so sorry
BRIANNA: Um, now's not really the ti—
JULES: **I'm REALLY REALLY**
So so SO so sorry
I was awful I ruined your life
EDNA: No, Jules, I'm …
So so SO so sorry
BRIANNA: SHHH! Guys!
EDNA: That your parents broke up
JULES: NO! I'M …
So so SO so sorry
For being a total—
BRIANNA: GUYS!

They remember where they are.

ALL: **OH MY AC-TU-AL GOD!**

JULES: **Jesus. Jesus. Jesus. Jesus. Jesus. Jesus.** [*Repeating*]

EDNA: **/ Je-sus. Jesus Christ. On a bike.** [*Repeating*]

BRIANNA: **/ THINK! THINK! We need to THINK! We need to— WAIT!**

JULES & EDNA: What?

BRIANNA: **Does he know, where he is?**

JULES & EDNA: Why?

BRIANNA: **Does he know?**

EDNA: No …

BRIANNA: So!
Why don't we just go and drug him?
And lay him down in the woods?

JULES: What?!
What the HELL is 'The Woods'?

BRIANNA: **Ahhhhh …**

JULES: **Where the HELL is 'The Woods'?**

BRIANNA: **Just a place that's far?**

JULES: **How the hell even WOULD we get him to the WOODS?**

EDNA: **I can drive and I have a car.**
I mean a van, but yeah—

JULES *and* BRIANNA *stare at something behind* EDNA. *Terrified. It's* CAROLINE.

CAROLINE: Eddy?

EDNA: Mum?

CAROLINE: Eddy.

EDNA: Mum.

CAROLINE: You are not driving anywhere.

Long pause.

I'll drive.
C'mon, girls.
Let's roll him up in the rug.

Blackout.

SCENE 13—TWO YEARS LATER

Lights up on LILY. *She's two years older.*

SONG: 'NOBODY REPRISE'

INTRO

LILY: **I was twelve when it happened.**
Never been the same
Read the news as I woke up
Till then I'd never known true pain
I couldn't eat

More FANS *appear. All two years older.*

SALTY: **I couldn't stop eating**
LILY: **I couldn't sleep**
SALTY: **I just couldn't even**
GRETA: **I could barely watch the footage**
DOM: **Felt like a kick to the head**
LILY: **He'd always been mine**
SALTY: **And now he was dead**

Everyone looks at SALTY, *confused.*

… Well, not literally dead, but ...
METAPHORICALLY
'Cause if you say that SHIT …
Then you're dead to MEEEE!

ALL: **He opened his mouth**
And opened our eyes
How could he do this to us?
How could he tell these lies?

The beat drops.

VERSE 1

DOM: **His story was so fake it was embarrassing**
I mean, how could a fourteen-year-old fan just kidnap him? LOL!
LILY: **How would she drive?**

Steal a van? Just—

GRETA: **Get past security?**

Take out the cameras?

ASH: **Then get to his dressing room, dressed as a roadie**

DOM: **Hide in his bathroom, wait till he does a poop**

LILY: **Knock him out with homemade chloroform**

GRETA: **Stuff him in a suitcase …**

LILY & GRETA: **And roll him out of the venue**

ALL: As if!

The VIDEO FAN CHORUS *all re-appear in the projection and sing backup.*

FANS: **As if!**

SALTY: **He said she tied him up, for two whole days**

FANS: **What the hell!**

SALTY: **That he screamed but no-one heard him**

Ummmmm-kay?

FANS: **Ummm kayyyy**

GRETA: **IT'S LIKE A BAD FAN FICTION!**

SALTY: What?

ALL: **Serious-laayy!**

LILY: Harry? I could write better crap than that!

ALL BUT SALTY: **Haarryyyyyy**

Eat a dick LITERALLY!

VERSE 2

DOM: **A week after they found him, to celebrate**

ASH: **They released a new single!**

GRETA: [*happy*] **LIKE NOTHING HAD CHANGED!**

SALTY: **His first night back onstage**

Something was … wrong

LILY: **He walked off after half a song**

ALL: **And never walked back on**

GRETA *and* DOM *leave.*

VERSE 3

LILY: **Some people said it was our fault**

Because teenage girls

Were all that's
Wrong with the world

ASH: **And is it weird to say I'm grateful**
That it happened, in a way?
The hateful garbage
It made me claim / what

SALTY: **What I'm not afraid to stand for**
That I am not afraid to looooove

VERSE 4

SALTY: **I still listen to that music**
I don't care what people say
I love how it feels to love it
And not feel afraid

LILY: **I still watch videos of the concerts**
Not to remember the boys
To remember how it felt to SCREAM
Inside all the noise

ASH: **Forget the overpriced tickets**
The merch, and the ugg boots

ASH & SALTY: **That's not why I loved that band**

ASH, LILY & SALTY: **It was a feeling, of throwing my hands up,**
And falling in love with life
And never having to land

They leave. EDNA *appears. Two years older.*

SONG: 'MAYBE WE'RE MORE'

VERSE 1

EDNA: **On the fourth day of high school**
Heading home all alone on the bus

BRIANNA *appears. Relaxed. Happy. She takes* EDNA*'s hand.*

BRIANNA: **That first afternoon when we met**

JULES *appears and takes* EDNA*'s other hand. They are best friends.*

JULES: **We could never have guessed**

What would happen to us
I got scared, didn't know how to act
BRIANNA: **I got scared my chest was too flat**
EDNA, JULES & BRIANNA: **But then I almost went to prison**

Two bars empty bars.

They blink.

So now I don't really care about that!

A banger synth. They dance like happy idiots.

CHORUS 1

ALL: **This world**
Is messy and cruel
And always tryna tell us
What. We. Should. Be. But—
Maybe we're more
Than silly little girls
Oh, just you wait. And—

VERSE 2

JULES: **We were tryna win a competition**
That we never asked to be in
BRIANNA: **Because the world told us we're never enough**
So we got stuck in trusting we were just disgusting, but—
EDNA: **Though this world**

SALTY *joins them.*

BRIANNA, JULES & SALTY: **Is messy and cruel**
EDNA: **We built one that's better**
And now I know
Thanks to you that—

CAROLINE *joins them.*

CAROLINE & EDNA: **It's a brave thing to love**
EDNA: **And the bravest thing, you can do**
Is to decide, you are already enough
And let nobody take that
From you

LILY *and* HARRY *join.*

CHORUS 2

ALL: **This world**
Is messy and cruel
HARRY: **And always tryna tell us.**
ALL: **What. We. Should. Be. But—**
Maybe we're more
Than silly little girls
Oh, just you wait. and—
ENSEMBLE: **Seeeeeee**

BUILD-UP

JULES: **If love hurts**
ALL: It doesn't make it real!
BRIANNA: **It just means you might get**
ALL: PTSD!
EDNA: **I don't need to be in love to feel loved**
ALL: **Or like someone that I wanna beeeee**
BRIANNA: I hope that the police never track us down!
ALL: **But let's just wait**
Let's just wait and seeeeee
JULES: **For now let's just enjoy the fact that you**
BRIANNA: **And you**
EDNA: **And y—**

A never-ending riff from LILY *like at the start.*

LILY: **You-u-u-u-u-u-u-o-woah**
ALL: **Are**
FREEEEEEEEEE

Their gospel chord turns into a squeal.

THE END

How *FANGIRLS* got made: A Q&A with Yve Blake and Jonathan Ware

YB: When *FANGIRLS* premiered in 2019, I was contacted by a lot of teenagers who wanted to know *how* the show was made.

I remember being that teenager, and so does my dramaturg, Jonathan Ware. So we decided to use the following pages to answer some of the best questions I got, and to shed some light on the five-year journey of bringing this show to life.

How long did it take to make *FANGIRLS*?

YB: I started researching it in January 2015, started writing it in April 2016, it opened in September 2019, and then I re-drafted it in June 2020 … so … five-plus years?

How did you learn how to write?

YB: I started writing plays when I was a teenager (the key word being 'started', I never finished anything), and then eventually I started using scenes I'd written to apply for playwriting groups and workshops. I never formally 'trained' in playwriting or songwriting at a university, I've just read/watched/listened to a lot of plays and musicals, and put in hours of practice. My main tips are: start writing before you feel 'ready', read every script you can get your hands on and accept that every first draft is *supposed* to be terrible.

What got you interested in writing about fangirls?

YB: In 2015, a member of the boy band One Direction (Zayn Malik) suddenly announced that he was leaving the band. I remember seeing mainstream news outlets report the story, and describing his fans as 'hysterical', 'hormonal', and likening them to 'banshees'. I noticed how gendered this language was, and I thought to myself, wait, why is it that the image of young girls screaming at a pop concert is often perceived as 'psycho', 'crazy', 'pathetic' or a 'bit much', but the image of a young boys screaming at a football match is often perceived as 'loyal' and 'passionate'? From that moment, I knew I wanted to write a show about fangirls. Because to me, the gendered way that the world talks about fangirls is a microcosm of how the world tries to minimise young women by undermining their intelligence and painting them as 'too emotional'.

What research did you do as a writer?

YB: My main area of research was the fandom of One Direction. I inhaled a bajillion tweets, tumblr posts, fan-made videos, vlogs, fan fics, conspiracy theories, DIY fan-art tutorials and interviewed loads of real life fans. Also, I taught a lot of drama workshops for teenagers while writing the show and ended up getting very inspired by things that my students would say.

What was your artistic goal when writing this show?

YB: It would have been too easy to simply write a show that *only* made fun of fangirls (or *only* defended them) so instead, I decided to make the show like a trojan horse. At the beginning, the show just looks like a comedy that invites you to laugh at teenage girls, but then! Bam! The show sneaks up on you and smuggles these girls into your heart.

I did this because I wanted to make a show that was truly for all generations. Whenever I went to the theatre as a teenager, I would notice that I was often the youngest person in the audience. Let's be real, lots of theatre is made to suit the tastes of old, rich, mostly white people. I wanted *FANGIRLS* to be a show where teenagers felt like they had *full* permission to be there.

Musically, I wanted the whole show to feel as adrenaline filled as a first crush, but I also wanted the score to contain moments of quiet beauty and give the audience the same goosebumps that the fans feel about Harry. Therefore, I wanted the show to sound like a 'pop concert meets rave meets church'.

Finally, I wanted the show to feel 'true'. I grew up watching TV shows where teenagers were played by hot 30-year-olds, and so I wanted the teenagers in *FANGIRLS* to be like I was as a teenager: awkward, and a bit feral. I wanted the lyrics to reflect the speed-of-light pace at which teenagers speak, I wanted to put the internet on stage, and I wanted to make a show that teenage me would not have found boring.

What instrument did you write the show on?

YB: I can't play any instruments, so I write all my songs on my computer. I use a program called Ableton Live, which I taught myself how to use off YouTube. When I need to put a melody or some chords into my computer, I hum each individual note and then press different letters on my qwerty keyboard until I find the note that matches the one in my head. If I can write a two-and-a-half-hour musical this way, anybody can do anything.

What's a dramaturg?

JW: A dramaturg can be a million different things depending on the project and the creatives you're working with. Whatever the project, it always involves responding to and providing feedback on work created by other artists—writers, designers, composers, choreographers, etc.

On *FANGIRLS*, I was part book editor, working with Yve on story development and script editing, and part resident musicologist, working with Yve and with David Muratore (Music Producer) and Alice Chance (Vocal Arranger) on theme, motif and lots of other musical elements to the show.

How does someone become a dramaturg?

JW: Again, a million different ways. I trained as a stage manager, and after working primarily on new works, I realised I was always interested in how stories are constructed. I then completed a Dramaturgy Masters at Victorian College of the Arts, focusing on dramaturgy for musicals, and particularly on how music adds another level to theatrical storytelling by accessing different parts of the audience's hearts and minds.

What research did you do as a dramaturg?

JW: For research, I looked at other musicals dealing with fandom and celebrity. My first reference was a show called *Bye Bye Birdie* (1960). It covers similar material to *FANGIRLS*, but has some outdated views on gender, and on the frivolity of fandom. During the *FANGIRLS* process, I often kept it in my mind as a guiding star of what NOT to do (sorry writers of *Bye Bye Birdie*!). Another reference was *Dreamgirls* (1981), which is a stage musical that moves at a whiplash pace that feels almost cinematic. For example, that show uses songs as montages, and will often put multiple locations on stage at once, like a split-screen device in a film. We knew that we wanted to use similar devices in *FANGIRLS*, and to make a musical that felt as fast-paced adrenaline-filled as a blockbuster film. We used some of the pacing devices of a blockbuster: jump cuts, dissolves and split-screens. These create a more cinematic storytelling mode, rather than the stop start of scene/song/scene in a more traditional musical theatre text.

How did you actually *start* writing this show? What part came first?

YB: I started with a very basic idea for the story: a fourteen-year-old girl is in love with the biggest pop star in the world, and goes to extreme lengths to meet him (see plot twist at the end of Act One). Before I could start writing any scenes or songs, I wrote a few drafts of the show's 'plot'. There were literally just paragraphs of what the story of the show might become, which included which bits of the story might give way to song.

JW: Sometimes this is called 'song-spotting'. Some of the songs Yve initially 'spotted' were:

- a 'Love Duet' between Edna and Harry (which became 'Let Them')
- an opening number for the fandom that we called 'Worship' (which turned into 'Nobody')
- an 'I Want' song for Edna ('Wait and See')
- 'Don't Exist' (kept its title!)
- and 'Justice', which was about fans uniting and calling out sexism (also kept its title)

Yve also 'spotted' lots of songs that later got cut, and some songs in the final show were only added much later.

YB: Once I had some song ideas, I wrote what I call a 'scaffold'. It's the whole show in dot point form. I use this step to plan out the structure of the show and also to figure out what I want the audience to learn in each scene/song. For example:

Scene One

- *Edna and Harry are on the run and escape the cops.*
- *Song: 'Love Duet'*
    - *Edna and Harry sing about their love. It's HOT.*
    - *We learn that they were unhappy before they found each other.*

Scene Two

- *Psych! That was a fan fic. Edna's mum interrupts her, is annoying.*
    - *We learn that Edna is actually a teenager, and on a scholarship.*
    - *We see that her mum is a nurse/shift worker.*

I showed this scaffold draft to Johnny and he helped me identify points where I was repeating information or the story was too slow. After redrafting my scaffold a few times, I could start writing the scenes and songs, because I knew what info they each needed to contain.

What was your process for writing the songs?

YB: To write the lyrics, I did lots of 'free-writing'. It's where you write a messy stream of consciousness without pausing or editing. I free-wrote pages of random lyrics about the themes of the show, and then together, Johnny and I highlighted all our favourite lines so that I could use them somewhere later (stuff like 'We want justice, Harry, and your kneecaps').

I composed the music in a similar way. I would make a *stack* of little musical 'loops' on my laptop (e.g. just sixteen seconds of a church organ playing four chords). Then, to build the songs, I would listen to my favourite loops on repeat and sing my favourite lyric bits over the top of them until something stuck. Eventually, I'd cobble together a first draft of a song that had five too many verses, and then I'd send that to Johnny and ask him what to cut.

For this show, I then took my redrafted songs to a music producer (David Muratore), who expanded my rough tracks and made them sound like real pop songs. I also collaborated with a Vocal Arranger (Alice Chance), who added rich vocal harmonies to the score.

How does a dramaturg help shape the songs?

JW: For this show, because we wanted the story to move at a rapid pace, I would constantly encourage Yve to avoid repeating information in her lyrics. This was challenging, given that Yve's score was inspired by pop music, in which songs often use a lot of repetition on purpose. In a musical though, songs need to be just as informative as scenes, so every line of a song should give the audience a new piece of information.

What was the biggest difference between the first draft and the final script?

JW: From the start, Yve was pretty clear about what happened in Act One, but Act Two changed a lot. The show's ending changed about seven times. The original ending involved a lot of blood.

YB: To be completely honest, I originally thought that the show needed to have a tragic ending where Edna … didn't survive. I wanted a shock ending that was all about the destructive cost of the lies we tell young women about themselves. But then I changed my mind. I decided that it was more powerful to write a story where Edna got her power back. I also wanted the audience to see Edna finally choosing to collaborate with the women in her life rather than fighting against them.

JW: We also had to cut lots of stuff which was fun but not essential to the story. Sometimes this is called 'killing your darlings'.

What 'darlings' did you have to kill?

YB: So so so so so so many. There are maybe hundreds of fun lines that didn't make the cut. One of my faves was: 'You know me and we haven't met, so I bought your spit on the internet'. RIP.

JW: Also there used to be a fourth friend at school called Sophie. And Edna's mum used to only be a voice we heard from offstage. A lot changed.

How did you actually get your show produced?

YB: This show really got made through word of mouth. In 2016, I began writing the show after winning a grant called the Rebel Wilson Theatre-Maker Scholarship (awarded by the Australian Theatre for Young People, or ATYP). That year, I began sending rough drafts of the tracks (with me singing all the parts) to industry mentors, to peers, and to potential producers, which was a really helpful way to build interest in it. At the end of 2016, I pulled together a live 45-minute 'showcase' of *FANGIRLS*, which I shared with an invited industry audience at ATYP. It consisted of seven extraordinary actresses singing the hell out of six draft songs from the show. Between each song, I talked to the crowd about the show's inspiration, its story, and what I hoped it would become. Crucially, ATYP got that showcase professionally filmed, and then sent the footage to every fancy producer who wasn't able to attend. Within a couple of weeks I was being approached by interested theatre companies, but it took another eighteen months of negotiations before I was handed a contract for the show to be made! My tips are: find cheap ways to put your work in front of people, film everything, and don't quit your bar job.

Did you do any readings of the script before you started rehearsals?

YB: *So many!* And these were all crucial to the show's development. Once Belvoir and Queensland Theatre licensed the show, we did two professional, week-long workshops of the show before rehearsals began. These involved a cast of actors reading and singing the show around a table, so that Johnny (Dramaturg), Paige (Director), Louise Gough (head of New Work at Belvoir) and I could make edits. However, before any producers were attached, I spent two-and-a-half years independently hustling to find opportunities to develop the show, and getting my mates to read it out loud around my dinner table. In this time I was lucky to get a week-long residency at The Barbican Open Lab in London, and then a week-long workshop of the show at the Adelaide Cabaret Festival, as well as funded showcases in London and Brisbane with the Women of the World Festival and in LA with the Australian Theatre Company. All up I must have re-drafted the show about twenty to thirty times.

What was the hardest part of the process? And what was the most fun part?

YB: The hardest part was staying patient and persistent. There were so many times when finishing this show felt impossible, and I felt like a 'bad' writer with 'bad' ideas. But the most fun part was the overwhelming response to the show. When the show opened in Brisbane and Sydney in 2019, I would look out at the audience and see so many young faces. I saw teenagers dancing in their seats next to their grandmas. I saw crying dads. I met teenagers in the foyer who had returned to see the show five times, and even some who had driven from Brisbane to Sydney to catch the show again. The cast received hand-made crafts inspired by the show, and started getting tagged in fan art (and fan-made memes)! By the end of our run in Sydney, we were so sold out that Belvoir began selling standing-room tickets, and when all of those tickets sold out, even I couldn't get more tickets. The energy in the audience was electric. Like a pop concert.

Any advice for aspiring writers or theatremakers?

YB: This job is only as fun as you make it, so don't beat yourself up too much with perfectionism. It's just glorified conformity. And also, no-one becomes a writer for the money, so at the end of the day, all you have in this job is your relationships to your collaborators and your peers. Therefore, be good to people. Praise your collaborators. Celebrate other writers. And remember to say thank you to all the people who help you along the way.

Yve Blake (Playwright)
Jonathan Ware (Dramaturg)